W9-AMB-090

# THE SEVEN PRINCIPLES
# IN ACTION

# THE SEVEN PRINCIPLES IN ACTION

*Improving Undergraduate Education*

Susan Rickey Hatfield, Editor
with
David G. Brown
Darrell W. Krueger
Susan J. Poulsen
Robert A. Scott
and special sections by
Martin Nemko, Contributing Editor

**Anker Publishing Company, Inc.**
Bolton, MA

THE SEVEN PRINCIPLES IN ACTION
*Improving Undergraduate Education*

ISBN 1–882982–05–3


Composition by Deerfoot Studios.
Cover design by Deerfoot Studios.


Anker Publishing Company, Inc.
176 Ballville Road
P.O. Box 249
Bolton, MA 01740–0249

# CONTENTS

# EDITORIAL INTRODUCTION

The Seven Principles for Good Practice in Undergraduate Education has attracted a great deal of attention since first published in 1987 in the *AAHE Bulletin*. How could anything as complex as an undergraduate education be improved by a list of ideas so short and simply stated that it can live on a card in your wallet? In their brevity lies an elegance, communicating the essence of effective practice in accelerating student achievement in higher education.

This book, edited by Susan Rickey Hatfield, Professor and Chair of Communication Studies at Winona State University, contains essays about the Seven Principles and abundant, specific and concrete examples of how they have been applied in scores of colleges and universities, large and small, public and private, throughout the United States and Canada. Also contained in this book are faculty, institutional and student inventories which provide vehicles for self-assessment of behaviors, policies, and practices for consistency with the Seven Principles.

Included in the book is a special supplement by Martin Nemko—educator, author, and advisor to institutions, students, and parents. The supplement is written to help parents and students use the Seven Principles as a guide in the selection of an undergraduate college or university. In his very personal and provocative style, Marty offers up a list of questions that students and parents must ask when choosing a college.

The editors gratefully acknowledge the assistance and support of The Johnson Foundation for continuing to support the Seven Principles for Good Practice in Undergraduate Education. In April, 1991, The Johnson Foundation—along with Winona State University, Ramapo College of New Jersey, and Wake Forest University—sponsored a conference on Improving Undergraduate Education: The Seven Principles in Action. This book emerged from that conference. The editors are indebted to Charles W. Bray, president of The Johnson Foundation.

The editors are also grateful for support from the Council of Public Liberal Arts Colleges without which this book could not have become a reality. The council is a consortium of small public colleges and universities that have, at their cores, both the liberal arts and a commitment to student-centered education. These institutions—The College of Charleston, The Evergreen State College, Keene State College, Mary Washington College, Northeast Missouri State University, Ramapo College of New Jersey, University of Minnesota–Morris, University of Maine–Farmington, and University of North Carolina–Asheville—exemplify, in their philosophy and in many of their programs, the Seven Principles in action.

Winona State University has been unflagging in its efforts to advance acceptance of The Seven Principles. As a quality-focused university, Winona State is applying the Seven Principles widely through its academic and residential programs. The university created the national Seven Principles Resource Center with generous support from the Winona State University Foundation. In addition, the university provided the editorial services of Susan Hatfield, without which this book would not have been possible.

The editors deeply appreciate the contribution of The Association of American Colleges and Universities (AAC&U). Excerpts from *Liberal Education* used herein are copyrighted by AAC&U and appear with permission. Further, David Stearman, former editor of *Liberal Education* and Theodore J. Marchese, executive editor of *Change* and Vice President of the American Association for Higher Education, rendered invaluable assistance in providing critical reading of the manuscript. And the editors wish to credit *Models II: Collaboration in Post Secondary Education*, edited by Anita Landau and Jill Mattuck Tarule, and *The Teaching Professor*, edited by Maryellen Weimer. Susan J. Collie served as the Editorial Assistant in the preparation of the manuscript.

Finally, but by no means last, the editors wish to thank each of the authors of the chapters of this book for their unstinting efforts and unwavering belief that this book will make a difference in the way in which undergraduates are taught and how effectively they learn.

John E. Ross
Institute for Effective Teaching
Winona, Minnesota

# PREFACE

Think back to the day you went off to college. What did you hope for in your college experience? Many college-bound students' expectations are embodied in Chickering and Gamson's *Seven Principles for Good Practice in Undergraduate Education*. Since their introduction in 1987, these principles have had an unprecedented response from the higher education community. In an 18-month period, 150,000 copies were ordered from The Johnson Foundation in Racine, Wisconsin.

The Seven Principles are not new. In an American Association for Higher Education address, Tom Angelo pointed out that 350 years ago, Comenius called for active learning: "Let the main object of our didactic be to seek and find a method of instruction by which teachers may teach less so that learners may learn more." What's new is the growing body of research supporting the importance of these principles, and their codification into an easy-to-remember format.

To date, despite being ever more validated, easy to remember, and widely disseminated, the Seven Principles have not been widely implemented. For instance, most faculty agree in the abstract that active learning is usually better than passive learning. Unfortunately if you walk down the halls of most undergraduate classroom buildings, you'll see that even in small classes, the dominant mode of instruction is passive: lecture, occasionally punctuated by questions.

One reason few professors implement active learning is that in planning their courses, they focus on transmitting masses of content and rarely consider the larger purposes of education. Another inhibitor to implementing active learning strategies is faculty generally teach the way they were taught, which was predominantly lecture/discussion. This stasis will likely persist as long as higher education continues its absurd practice of de-emphasizing teaching in preparing, hiring, and rewarding faculty members. Ernest Boyer has noted, "I would like to hear, at least occasionally, 'Teach or Perish'." Imagine a similar situation with surgeons. Would you want to be operated on by a surgeon who received little or no training in how to perform surgery, got hired primarily based on potential to publish journal articles, and was retained and promoted with little regard to how many of his patients died?

A third reason for the heretofore limited implementation—not just of active learning but of all the Seven Principles—is that educational institutions are like motels: most faculty members have no idea what's going on in the next room. This book is designed to help break down the walls between the rooms, to describe common sense, practical ways that faculty and administrators around the country are implementing the Seven Principles. Authors of chapters in this book describe how the Seven Principles are being used, not only at their own colleges but also at other institutions around the country—two year as well as four year, public and private, large and small.

The rich and extensive lists of possibilities should provide ready ideas for all professors. This isn't a theoretical book. It is, instead, a practical resource book for getting good practices in undergraduate education into the classroom. Its menu of ideas is varied, diverse, cross-curricular, and imaginative.

In the hope of initiating a support network, we have included our phone numbers, as well as those of faculty who are putting the Seven Principles into action. We also invite you to send comments or other examples of the Seven Principles at work for use at the Seven Principles Resource Center, Winona State University, Winona, MN 55987.

The Seven Principles also offer students a rationale for selecting a college or university. To that end, I have developed a special section, "How to Choose a College", including a College Report Card, based in part on the Seven Principles. Following this is a related section on "How to Test-Drive a College."

We hope that this book will be a resource for all of us who work to ensure that, as students go off to college, their hopes are fulfilled.

Martin Nemko

*Martin Nemko is the author of* How to Get an Ivy League Education at a State University, *which profiles the undergraduate programs at 115 public colleges and universities. His firm, Nemko & Associates, Oakland, CA, assists administrators in developing and evaluating undergraduate programs.*

# INTRODUCTION

## THE SEVEN PRINCIPLES FOR GOOD PRACTICE IN UNDERGRADUATE EDUCATION: A HISTORICAL PERSPECTIVE

*Zelda F. Gamson*

The Seven Principles for Good Practice in Undergraduate Education distills findings from decades of research on the undergraduate experience into seven basic principles. These principles, which are based on a view of education as active, cooperative, and demanding, assert that good practice in undergraduate education:

1. encourages student-faculty contact

2. encourages cooperation among students

3. encourages active learning

4. gives prompt feedback

5. emphasizes time on task

6. communicates high expectations

7. respects diverse talents and ways of learning

## The Origins of the Seven Principles Project

The Seven Principles are the result of a complex series of activities. As one of seven members of the Study Group on the Conditions of Excellence in Undergraduate Education that produced *Involvement in Learning* (Study Group on the Conditions of Excellence in American Higher Education, 1984)—the first in a series of reports on undergraduate education in the 1980's (Bennett, 1984; Association of American Colleges, 1985; Newman, 1985; Boyer, 1987)—I feared that these reports would fail to reach the faculty members, administrators, and students to whom they were directed. When I joined the Board of the American Association for Higher Education (AAHE) in the middle 1980s, I participated in the decision to embark on a series of conferences on the improvement of undergraduate education. In the discussion that led to this decision, I suggested that AAHE sponsor the development of a statement of principles for a good undergraduate education. Arthur Chickering, also a member of the AAHE Board, agreed to work with me on a plan to do so.

A few months after the AAHE board meeting, where we discussed the need for principles to guide the improvement of undergraduate education, Chickering and I attended a conference at Wingspread, the conference center in Racine, Wisconsin operated by The Johnson Foundation. This conference brought together the authors of several of the recent reports on undergraduate education, along with a number of other observers of higher education. It was clear to Chickering and me that a statement of principles, widely disseminated to the academic community, could be an important next step in the education reform movement that was sweeping the country.

How were we to generate such a statement? We wanted the principles to represent the collective wisdom of colleagues who were knowledgeable about the research literature on the college experience. With support from The Johnson Foundation, we invited a small task force to meet for two days at Wingspread in July, 1986. The task force members included scholars who had contributed much of the research on the impact of the college experience over the last five decades, as well as other students of higher education: Alexander W. Astin of UCLA, Howard Bowen of the Claremont Colleges, William Boyd of The Johnson Foundation,

Carol M. Boyer of the Education Commission of the States (a co-sponsor of the conference), K. Patricia Cross of Harvard, Kenneth Eble of the University of Utah, Russell Edgerton of AAHE (a co-sponsor of the conference), Jerry Gaff of Hamline University, Henry Halsted of The Johnson Foundation, Joseph Katz of SUNY-Stony Brook, C. Robert Pace of UCLA, Marvin Peterson of the University of Michigan, and Richard C. Richardson, Jr. of Arizona State University.

The gathering was an extraordinary event in its own right. Most of the members of the task force were acquainted with one another and knew each other's work, but they had never all met together to trace the implications of their research for the improvement of undergraduate education. Chickering and I set them a difficult task. As the call to the meeting put it, scholars of higher education will meet "to identify key principles which characterize the practices of educationally successful undergraduate institutions. Conferees will identify research which supports those characteristics and create a draft statement of principles." Chickering and I asked the participants to react to a list of eight principles which we had drawn up ahead of time, with the caveat that they were to end up with no more than nine principles, preferably fewer. Mindful of psychological research showing that most people can hold in mind between five and nine discrete items at a time, we were determined to avoid the temptation of a long laundry list of principles, even if that meant neglecting some crucial areas.

Chickering and I insisted that whatever we produce be accessible, understandable, practical, and widely applicable. We hoped to be able to get the principles on a single page, easily and cheaply produced, and even joked about a "pocket" version that administrators and faculty members could whip out at a moment's notice. The group was sensitive about the principles being misapplied by faculty members and misused by state agencies in their effort to make higher education more accountable. This concern provoked a good deal of discussion about the audiences for the eventual principles. While everyone agreed that faculty members were the most important audience—and the primary audience for Chickering and me—several task force members felt strongly that they should try to reach campus administrators, state higher education agencies, and government policy makers.

These multiple audiences increased the complexity of the task of framing the principles.

A series of drafts criss-crossed the country, following members of the task force at home, work, and vacation. As the final draft began to take shape, Chickering and I suggested that the principles be directed primarily to faculty members in their roles as teachers, but that we also try to reach a broader audience of administrators and policy makers whose support would be necessary for the principles to take hold. A statement, which appeared in the original Principles document as "Whose Responsibility Is It?" addressed administrators about what they needed to do to encourage good practice in their institutions and urged policymakers to help campuses improve undergraduate education.

The final version of the Seven Principles for Good Practice in Undergraduate Education appeared as the lead article in the March 1987 issue of the *AAHE Bulletin* (Chickering and Gamson, 1987). It began by drawing attention to criticisms of undergraduate education and moved quickly to an emphasis on campus-level improvement, listing the Seven Principles and then describing them in greater detail, with practical examples from a variety of campuses. The response to the article was immediate, and plans began soon after to re-publish it as a special section in the June 1987 issue of *The Wingspread Journal,* a publication of The Johnson Foundation. With the help of Susan J. Poulsen, Director of Public Communications at The Johnson Foundation, the re-published version was designed for visual appeal and accessibility.

And they were ordered! More than 150,000 copies of the Seven Principles were ordered directly from The Johnson Foundation over the next 18 months from colleges and universities throughout the U.S., as well as from Canada, the United Kingdom, and several other countries. An unknown number were copied or reprinted in other publications, such as the newsletters of the American Association of State Colleges and Universities and centers for teaching improvement at colleges and universities across the country (the Seven Principles were not copyrighted). A version of the principles was published in *University Affairs,* a news magazine on higher education in Canada. Chickering and I conducted workshops and conference sessions using the Seven Principles, asking participants to discuss how they might implement them.

## The Inventories

The enthusiastic response to the Seven Principles encouraged us to develop a self-assessment instrument for faculty members, with examples and indicators of each of the principles. In keeping with the task force's recognition that even the most sophisticated, motivated faculty members needed institutional support for serious attention to teaching, we also concentrated on producing an institutional inventory, with indicators of campus practices and policies in support of the Seven Principles. With a small grant from the Lilly Endowment, we began the arduous task of selecting a small number from among the hundreds of examples of the principles from participants in workshops, from other instruments, from publications, and from our own experience. Louis Barsi, then a graduate student at George Mason University, joined us at this stage.

The final version of each inventory was designed and published in the fall of 1989 by The Johnson Foundation in two handy self-assessment booklets. The indicators in the Faculty Inventory are divided into seven sections, one for each principle. The indicators in the Institutional Inventory are divided into six sections that support good practices in undergraduate education: Climate, Academic Practices, Curriculum, Faculty, Support Services, and Facilities. Announcements of the availability of the Inventories were placed in The Johnson Foundation's *Wingspread Journal* and the newsletters of several national higher education associations, and an article was published in the November 1989 issue of the *AAHE Bulletin* (Gamson and Poulsen, 1989).

The response to the Inventories, available then at no cost, was overwhelming. Within a week, all 40,000 of the two Inventories printed by The Johnson Foundation were gone. With additional help from the Lilly Endowment, the Inventories went into a second printing. The response to the Principles and the Inventories was so astonishing that it occasioned an article in *The Chronicle of Higher Education* (Heller, 1989). A source book published in 1991 recounts the research support for the Seven Principles and draws on examples of how they have been used from a survey of institutions that requested the Seven Principles and Inventories early and from vignettes about a range of colleges and universities and a higher education association (Chickering and Gamson, 1991).

In *The Seven Principles in Action: Improving Undergraduate Education*, the authors have gathered an impressive compendium of how the seven principles are being used both across the curriculum and across the nation.

## Further Developments

Several groups have been working on adaptations of the Inventories. The Faculty Inventory has been adapted for use by students. This new Inventory will list student behaviors that contribute to the achievement of each of the principles. The Student Inventory was stimulated by William Coplin, Professor of Policy Studies and Public Affairs at Syracuse University. With financial support from The Johnson Foundation, Louis Barsi, Arthur Chickering, William Coplin and Susan Poulsen met in April 1990 with Brian Hand, an alumnus of a university in the Washington, D.C. area; Karen Romer, Associate Dean at Brown University; Cindy Ward, a college sophomore; and Maryellen Gleason Weimer, a researcher at Pennsylvania State University. This meeting laid out the general orientation for the Student Inventory.

The Seven Principles and Inventories are also being adapted for use in research and educational improvement overseas. Arthur Chickering has begun work with senior professors at the Université Lumière Lyon II and the Université Mendes Franco in Grenoble to adapt the Inventories for the French lycées. His project will involve professors at the two universities, administrators, and teachers in the lycées.

Another group, under the leadership of the Seven Principles Resource Center at Winona State University, has been adapting the Seven Principles to Total Quality Management approaches. At Wingspread in the fall of 1992, experienced practitioners of quality improvement in industry met faculty members and administrators from several colleges and universities around the country to explore this extension of the Seven Principles.

The Seven Principles project has been highly collaborative from its beginning. It has benefited from the help of several higher education associations and two foundations. It has built on the expertise of some of the leading scholars of higher education. Most important, it has drawn on the ideas of hundreds of faculty members and administrators in colleges and universities around the country.

In this new book, educators share their innovative implementations of the Seven Principles. This volume demonstrates the flexibility of the Seven Principles and provides myriad and diverse perspectives on how to put the principles into effective action.

A final note: the new Student Inventory is published by the Seven Principles Resource Center at Winona State University, which has taken over the production and distribution of the Seven Principles and Inventories. The Seven Principles Resource Center has established a resource library of materials relating to the use and effectiveness of the Seven Principles and Inventories. To order copies or obtain more information, contact:

> Seven Principles Resource Center
> Winona State University
> PO Box 5838
> Winona, MN 55987-5838
> (507) 457-5020
> Fax: (507) 457-5586

*Zelda F. Gamson is Founding Director of the New England Resource Center for Higher Education and Professor of Education at the University of Massachusetts at Boston.*

## References

Association of American Colleges. (1985). *Integrity in the College Curriculum: A Report to the Academic Community*. Washington, D.C.: Association of American Colleges.

Bennett, W. J. (1984). *To Reclaim a Legacy: A Report on the Humanities in Higher Education*. Washington, D.C.: National Endowment for the Humanities.

Boyer, E. L. (1987). *College: The Undergraduate Experience in America*. New York, NY: Harper and Row.

Chickering, A. W. and Gamson, Z. F. (1987). Seven principles for good practice in undergraduate education." *AAHE Bulletin*, 39 (7), 3–7.

Chickering, A. W. and Gamson, Z. F. (1991). Applying the seven principles for good practice in undergraduate education. *New Directions in Teaching and Learning*. No. 47, San Francisco: Jossey-Bass.

Gamson, Z. F., and Poulsen, S. J. (1989). Inventories of good practice: the next step for the seven principles for good practice in undergraduate education. *AAHE Bulletin*, 47 (3), 7–8, 14.

Heller, S. (1989). Delighted authors find their agenda for education is a huge hit. *Chronicle of Higher Education*, December 13, 1989, pp. A41, A43.

National Institute of Education. (1984). *Involvement in Learning: Realizing the Potential of American Higher Education.* Final report of the study group on the conditions of excellence in American higher education. Washington, DC: U.S. Department of Education News.

Newman, F. (1985). *Higher Education and the American Resurgence.* Princeton, NJ: Carnegie Foundation for the Advancement of Teaching.

**Principle 1: Good Practice Encourages Student-Faculty Contact**

*Frequent student-faculty contact in and out of classes is the most important factor in student motivation and involvement. Faculty concern helps students get through rough times and keep on working. Knowing a few faculty members well enhances students' intellectual commitment and encourages them to think about their own values and future plans.*

1

# GOOD PRACTICE ENCOURAGES STUDENT-FACULTY CONTACT

*Judith A. Sturnick and Keith J. Conners*

## Student-Faculty Contact: An Overview

The first of the Seven Principles for Good Practice in Undergraduate Education seems almost axiomatic, even to those unfamiliar with the rich body of research that supports the importance of student-faculty contact. That students tend to benefit from interaction with faculty is hardly surprising, and it is understandable that Arthur Chickering and Zelda Gamson listed student-faculty contact as the lead principle. Besides the ample research-based documentation of the importance of student-faculty interaction, there is also a wonderfully romanticized image of the ideal teacher-learner relationship embedded in our cultural traditions. Heroic depictions of teachers in literature, on film, and on television have reinforced the notion that magical connections between teachers and students can produce glorious academic achievement and transform lives.

Sometimes it works that way. All campuses have some inspired and inspiring faculty who leave indelible marks upon students. Indeed, anyone who has earned a degree or two can likely point to one or more especially influential teachers. Virtually every college values the interaction of students and faculty; one would be hard pressed to find a catalog or campus mission statement which did not include reference to this principle of good practice. The encouragement of student-faculty interaction is accorded especially high priority among smaller colleges and universities that focus on undergraduate education and that emphasize a broad-based liberal arts education.

It seems so simple: place students and faculty together and let the magic happen. Put every biology student shoulder-to-shoulder in the laboratory with a professor engaged in ground breaking research. Let every history student's essays be lovingly critiqued by an eminent scholar in the field. Encourage every English professor to recreate the Dead Poet's Society. Bring to life every viewbook picture that shows an animated coffee shop conversation among students and faculty after class. As the cost of college attendance escalates, students and parents will expect to seek real value in higher education, and the promise of meaningful student-faculty interaction takes on increased importance. Quite reasonably, the consumers of higher education want their share of the magic.

### Obstacles to Student-Faculty Contact

Unfortunately, there are obstacles—both real and perceived—to the goal of getting students and faculty together for regular, productive interaction. These barriers are not just created by faculty and students, but may also be created by the institution itself.

Managing in-class faculty-student discussions is difficult, even for those faculty most skilled at facilitating interaction. Outside of class, full-time faculty are often drawn away from extensive interaction with students by other legitimate expectations of the profession.

But students play a role in this too. Not all students feel comfortable participating in class discussions. Many are content to take a passive role in the learning process and don't value class discussion as an essential part of the learning experience. When faculty make themselves available to meet with students outside of class, students don't always take advantage of this opportunity. Other demands require students to move quickly from one class to the next obligation, ruling out time after class or during the day for extensive follow-up interaction with faculty. Finally, students might perceive some faculty as "unapproachable" and feel uncomfortable interacting with them in out-of-class situations.

A larger barrier to student-faculty contact may be either intentionally or unintentionally created by the universities. The layout and structure of academic buildings may not facilitate interaction. Faculty offices may be too small to host students. Potential lounge areas for students and faculty to meet may have been converted for other "more important" purposes. Even dining areas are delineated—either formally or informally—solely for students or faculty. In short, though many institutions give lip service to promoting student faculty interaction, the result is far short of the goal.

### *Overcoming the Obstacles*

It is safe to assume that every college and university sets goals and designs programs with the intention of fostering meaningful contact between students and faculty, yet there are campuses where student-faculty interaction is little more than a viewbook image for many students. Sometimes the barriers are circumstantial: part-time and commuter students do not have time to develop close relationships with faculty because employment and family responsibilities draw them off campus. One suspects, however, that on many campuses, the principle obstacle to extensive student-faculty interaction is the absence of an ethos which values teaching, advising, and a commitment to the student above all other faculty role expectations. A campus ethos which clearly supports and encourages faculty-student contact can help overcome many of the barriers outlined above.

*Faculty.* It is natural to think of traditional classroom and laboratory settings when student-faculty interaction is discussed. But many opportunities for meaningful contact among students and teachers occur outside of class, in both formal and informal situations. The principle of good practice which encourages student-faculty interaction assumes both academic and co-curricular formal and informal involvements between students and faculty. Indeed, there seems to be a high degree of correlation between faculty who maximize interaction with students in class and those who find meaningful interactions with students outside of class.

The substantial body of research on effective teaching, upon which most systems for evaluating college teaching are based, emphasizes teacher behavior that actively engages students in learning. In addition to other traits such as command of subject matter, clear communication of expectations, enthusiasm, and expressiveness, effective teachers are often identified as those who encourage classroom interaction, establish rapport with students, and provide individualized feedback and reinforcement of student performance. Good teachers are further described as approachable, interested in students' learning and well-being, accessible, open to students' ideas and questions, and concerned about students' progress.

Not surprisingly, those faculty who are most supportive of students' individual needs in the classroom and laboratory settings tend to be those to whom students turn outside of the class for academic and personal assistance. One important study on this topic (Wilson, et al., 1975) found that faculty who were cited by students and colleagues as especially effective teachers reported more interaction with students beyond the classroom than other faculty. Similarly, this multi-campus study found that students who reported gains in intellectual commitment, certainty of career choice, and satisfaction with academic and non-academic experiences during their college years reported more contact with faculty, particularly outside of class, than did other students.

In light of this, it seems obvious that the primary criteria in the hiring, promotion and tenure of faculty should be how faculty demonstrate their dedication to promoting interaction between themselves and their students. Interestingly enough, at many universities interaction with students weighs as little as 20% in such decisions.

*Students.* It would be misleading to assume that the obligation for increasing student-faculty interaction rests entirely on faculty. Quality undergraduate education depends upon the integration of students, faculty, and other members of the campus community. Students who arrive on campus determined to become active players in their campus community stand a much greater chance of benefiting from their college experience. College faculty members can be expected to reciprocate the vitality new students bring to the classroom every quarter or semester.

*University.* Finally, other obstacles to the student-faculty interaction may be overcome by careful attention to both campus structure and climate. Some campuses have been attentive to facility planning in ways that have encouraged student and faculty to cross paths regularly. Others offer special programs and encouragement for commuter students who might otherwise find themselves at a disadvantage when compared to residential students who live, eat, play, and study in close proximity to the faculty seven days a week. More significant than structural facilitation, though, is the difficult task of developing a campus ethos which supports and rewards faculty who make a commitment to students and provides students with the means and the encouragement to seek out faculty contact both in and out of class.

## Promoting Student-Faculty Contact: Two Examples

Keene State College in New Hampshire is one of several public liberal arts colleges which has made a priority of encouraging student-faculty interaction with gratifying results. Keene State has developed a number of programs—many of which have been successful on other campuses—which serve to maximize student-faculty interaction. Of particular note is the college's Freshman Year Experience Program (FYE), in which all first-year students enroll in a standard introductory discipline-based course identified as having an "FYE" section. The FYE designation indicates that the instructor of the course has teamed with an "FYE associate" from the campus community (deans, administrators, counselors, residence hall staff, carpenters, and secretaries have all served in this role) to determine how the course will meet the goals for the Freshman Year Experience Program. While the faculty member remains responsible for course content and student evaluation, the associate supplements class activities in a variety of ways: leading small group discussions, coordinating study sessions, facilitating library orientation, providing information about campus resources, and generally assisting both students and faculty throughout the semester.

Salisbury State University in Maryland has another approach to ensuring meaningful student-faculty interaction at the earliest stage of a student's enrollment. To supplement the standard freshman orientation seminar required of all students at SSU, about two dozen new students sign up for the "Algonquin Experience" during late August. Accompanied by faculty, staff, and upper-class student leaders, these students drive in vans to Ontario, Canada, and spend two weeks canoeing, camping, and preparing for life on campus in September. The relationships formed between students and faculty during this experience are among the richest of the students' undergraduate careers.

## Meaningful Student-Faculty Contact: The Principle in Action

Many institutions around the country are using creative ideas successfully to increase the amount of contact between faculty and students. The following examples provide ideas that private and public colleges and universities are using to increase faculty and student contact.

### First-year Student Programs

- From the outset, students at Grinnell College establish one-on-one contacts with faculty members. Faculty instructors serve as academic advisors to individual students during their Freshman Research and Writing Tutorials, and guide students in planning a two-year course of study in preparation for declaring a major.

  > Charles Duke, VP Academic Affairs and Dean of Faculty
  > Grinnell College, P. O. Box 805
  > Grinnell, IA 50112
  > (515) 269-3100

- All first-year students at Augsburg College are divided into groups of fifteen students and spend one hour per week during the fall semester discussing readings from an anthology created by faculty members. Each group is led by a faculty member who also serves as the academic advisor for students in that group.

  > Ryan LaHurd, VP Academic Affairs and Dean
  > Augsburg College, 731 21st Ave., So.
  > Minneapolis, MN 55454
  > (612) 330-1024

- "Each One, Reach One" is a special program at the College of Charleston in South Carolina for entering minority students.

Each new student is paired with a faculty or staff member or a senior student to provide personal contact on campus. Activities are planned for all students and mentors, and the mentors are encouraged to develop supportive activities on an individual basis.

> William Lindstrom, Dean of Undergraduate Studies
> College of Charleston
> 68 George Street
> Charleston, SC 29424
> (803) 953-5674

## Advising

Virtually every campus that values undergraduate education cites advising as a critical component in student retention and success. Some innovative advising approaches attempt to bring students and faculty (and often other professional staff) together in support of quality education.

- The University of Michigan-Flint found that academic advising was a component of student-faculty interaction which seemed to be slipping out of faculty hands. At the recommendation of a faculty committee, an Advising Center was created with the understanding that all new students—freshman and transfer—would be assigned to one of the specially trained faculty members holding an appointment at the Center. Besides the special training, faculty appointments involve a year-round obligation to the work of the Center in addition to regular faculty duties.

  > Advising Center
  > University of Michigan-Flint
  > Flint, MI 48502
  > (313) 762-3300

- In addition to promoting a campus climate that embraces individual differences, Pomona College also caters to the special needs of minority students. One way the college addresses the needs of African-American students is the faculty mentor program. The program was developed as a way to strengthen nonacademic ties between African-American students and faculty members. Students and faculty complete forms describing their interests, including the kinds of books they like to read, the kinds of cultural or athletic events they like to attend, and the kinds of activities they like to do. These forms are used to match students with mentors. In addition to providing close ties to the university, administrators hope that the program will encourage Pomona's African-American students to think about pursuing a career in academic life.

Toni Clark, Associate Dean of Students/Dean of Women
Pomona College, 550 N. College
Claremont, CA 91711
(909) 621-8017

- More undergraduates major in mathematics at the State University of New York College at Potsdam than at any other American university save one. The extraordinarily supportive program of instruction which emphasizes student-faculty interaction and a commitment to student success by math faculty are major reasons for this phenomenon. Careful mentoring and advising, small classes, supplemental instruction, and a tradition of innovative instructional practice by faculty are components of a remarkable program where over 300 students (on a campus just over 4000) major in mathematics.

Provost Dudly-Eshbach
SUNY Potsdam
Pierrepont Avenue
Potsdam, NY 13767
(315) 267-2108
FAX (315) 267-2496

## *Small Classes and Structural Enhancements*

In some cases instructors have worked to limit student-faculty ratios to improve student-faculty interaction, while others have focused on campus facility design and use of resources to maximize student contact with faculty:

- The Hutchins School of Liberal Studies at Sonoma State University in California provides a lower-division seminar with a class size of about 12 students. Meeting three times weekly for two hours, the seminar provides an intensive, interactive forum for students and faculty. Participating faculty members also serve as advisors, meeting students informally to plan programs as well as organizing individual and group projects and activities.

> Les Adler, Provost
> Hutchins School of Liberal Studies
> Sonoma State University
> Rohnert Park, CA 94928
> (707) 664-2491

- At Keene State College, students and faculty participate actively in campus master planning and new facility design. Hundreds of faculty and students were interviewed by the college's master planning consultants as designs were proposed for renovation and relocation of major campus facilities, as well as prioritizing the sequence of new buildings. Careful attention was paid to siting and functional uses of new residence halls, an art gallery, and a campus center to maximize interaction among students, faculty, and staff outside of class.

> Jay Kahn, Vice President for Finance & Planning
> Keene State College
> Keene, NH 03431
> (603) 358-2114

- The Western College Program at Miami University in Ohio takes advantage of the architecture of its main building to ensure a high degree of student-faculty interaction. Designed on the holistic model of women's colleges in the mid-nineteenth century, the facility contains faculty offices, classrooms, student rooms, residence hall common areas, a small library, and computer facilities all under one roof. This arrangement facilitates a 24-hour educational experience for students as faculty utilize offices and other resources in the building while doing their work among residential students. The setting allows for easy, unavoidable contact among students and faculty and fosters a unique learning environment for both.

> Curtis W. Ellison, Dean
> School of Interdisciplinary Studies
> Miami University
> 119 Peabody Hall
> Oxford, OH 45056
> (513) 529-5643

### Encouraging Student Interaction

Most universities have explicit expectations of the number of hours faculty should be available to students each week. Still, faculty find that students are hesitant to engage in one-on-one interaction during office hours.

- A York College (PA) professor encourages student turnout during office hours by placing an invitation within the course syllabi: "You are encouraged to stop in during office hours to talk about any problems or suggestions you may have concerning the course; about careers (especially graduate school, law school, or the benefits of majoring or minoring in political science); or just about politics or things in general. If you want to talk to me and find the schedule hours to be inconvenient, feel free to schedule an appointment."

    Mel Kulbicki
    Department of Political Science
    York College
    Country Club Road
    York, PA 17404
    (717) 846-7788

- To encourage faculty at Miami University to meet informally with their students outside of the classroom, the MU student Parent's Organization has set up a "Popcorn Fund." Available to all faculty at the university, the fund reimburses faculty $1 per student to cover the cost of providing refreshments at their out-of-class gatherings.

    Myrtis Powell, Vice President for Student Affairs
    Miami University
    Oxford, OH 45056
    (513) 529-1877

While many faculty are comfortable providing students with their home phone numbers, others find that e-mail allows students to have access to them beyond their posted office hours, while maintaining boundaries between professional and personal lives. Computer technology also allows student-faculty interaction to continue in cyberspace.

- Faculty at St. Norbert College, Wisconsin, develop electronic mail discussion groups in the International Relations class. Many instructors find students may be more willing to participate in a written discussion than to speak up during class. The instructor monitors the discussions and participates along with the students, adding personal perspectives and ideas to those of the students.

    Deborah Furlong
    Social Sciences
    St. Norbert College
    DePere, WI 54115
    (414) 337-3181

## Undergraduate Research Opportunities

Although research is traditionally thought of in conjunction with graduate education at major universities, a number of smaller, teaching-oriented undergraduate institutions have encouraged faculty and students to pursue high quality undergraduate research projects:

- The New College at the University of South Florida has emphasized student research and student-faculty interaction as the most effective means of learning. This approach is particularly apparent in its biology program, where students are encouraged to undertake intensive research projects in their freshman year.

    Sandra Gilchrist, Associate Professor of Biology
    New College of the University of South Florida
    Sarasota, FL 34243
    (813) 359-4377

- Iowa State University encourages the early introduction of freshmen Honors students to the research arena through a program designed to give bright freshmen a chance to become familiar with research and to serve as active partners with faculty in the process. The goal of the program is to have qualified undergraduate students engaged in significant research efforts during their careers at Iowa State.

Elizabeth C. Beck
Coordinator, University Honors Program
Iowa State University
Ames, IA
(515) 294-4371
FAX (515) 294-2970

On many campuses, special awards and recognition are provided for both students and faculty who participate in undergraduate research projects.

• At Keene State College, a chemistry professor secured a large National Science Foundation grant to purchase a highly specialized piece of equipment which the college could not have financed otherwise. He has used that acquisition not only as the basis for his own research but to draw a variety of undergraduate students into original research projects. As a result, papers have been read jointly by faculty and students at national meetings, and articles have been jointly published in scholarly journals. Going beyond the joint writing and research endeavors, however, this faculty member also uses the scholarly accomplishments to propel highly motivated students into the most prestigious graduate programs around the country, often helping them secure significant graduate fellowships on the basis of their research work.

Eleanor VanderHaegen, Dean of Sciences
Keene State College
Keene, NH 03431
(603) 358-2544

*Judith A. Sturnick is Granite State Professor, University System of New Hampshire, and former President of Keene State College.*

*Keith J. Conners is Professor, College of Education, Salisbury State University.*

## Resources: Student-Faculty Contact

Biology students learn by doing: University of South Florida. (1990). *Liberal Education*, 76 (4), 43–44.

Building awareness and diversity into student life: Pomona College. (1991). *Liberal Education*, 77 (1), 38–40.

First year experience creates a community of learners: Augsburg College. (1989). *Liberal Education,* 75 (5), 28–29.

Freedom of choice encourages active learning; Grinnell College. (1988). *Liberal Education,* 74 (4), 27–28.

Furlong, D. (1994). Using electronic mail to improve instruction. *The Teaching Professor,* 8( 6), 7.

Lamport, M. A. (1993). Student-faculty interaction and the effect on college student outcomes: A review of the literature. *Adolescence,* 28 (112), 971–990.

O'Neill, K. L. and Todd-Mancillas, W. R. (1992). An investigation into the types of turning points affecting relational change in student-faculty interactions. *Innovative Higher Education,* 16, (4), 227–290.

Wilson, R. C., Gaff, J. G., Dienst, L. W., and Bavry, J. L. (1975). *College Professors and Their Impact on Students.* New York, NY: John Wiley.

**Principle 2: Good Practice Encourages Cooperation Among Students**

*Learning is enhanced when it is more like a team effort than a solo race. Good learning, like good work, is collaborative and social, not competitive and isolated. Working with others often increases involvement in learning. Sharing one's own ideas and responding to others' reactions improves thinking and deepens understanding.*

# 2

# COOPERATIVE LEARNING COMMUNITIES

*Tim Hatfield and Susan Rickey Hatfield*

## Cooperative Learning: An Overview

In colleges and universities, as in the secondary schools which continue to provide them with the majority of their students, traditional practice has involved conscious efforts to stimulate competition among students in order to promote their learning. With honorable intentions, fueled by myths ranging from "competition is the best preparation a student can have for a survival of the fittest world" to "competition is a key builder of character", college classrooms have become places where competition reigns. By extension, these same colleges and universities are places where some students "win" and many students "lose." That is what competition is all about.

Unfortunately, it also is what too many college classrooms are all about, in spite of growing literature and case examples of the benefits of promoting cooperation rather than competition among students. The benefits of cooperative learning are broad indeed: individual student learning, group learning in and out of the classroom, and the promotion of a positive campus-wide learning community. Vincent Tinto, Anne Goodsell-Love and Pat Russo (1993) explored some of the effects of learning community experiences on first year students. Their study of two and four year colleges (*Building Learning Communities for New College Students: A Summary of Research Findings of the Collaborative Learning Project*) found that:

- Participation in the collaborative learning experience helps students form a small supportive group that eases the transition from high school to college and helps them integrate into the university.

- Learning communities help students bridge the gap between the institutions' academic and social cultures.

- Learning communities give students a sense of ownership of the learning process.

- Learning communities have a positive effect on persistence.

In this kind of a community, students care more about learning because of the interdependent nature of the process. Students retain more because there is both a social context and intellectual activity related to the subject matter. And students find the process understandably more enjoyable than the norm of competition in which the basic expectation is that a few students will shine while the rest hope that the curve isn't too severe.

Innumerable examples of supportive, cooperative, inclusive working/learning communities exist in the burgeoning quality literature. The examples reinforce what cooperative learning advocates have known for quite some time: cooperation, not competition, is more effective in promoting student learning.

## Cooperative Experiences

Many types of valuable cooperative-learning activities are applicable across disciplines.

*Group Projects, Presentations, Papers.* These are the most common cooperative learning activities, where a student group is responsible for the production of a particular product. Usually, the product is evaluated and serves as a basis for some percentage of each student's grade for the course. Audio, visual, and computer technologies have broadened the possibilities for these types of cooperative projects.

*Study Groups.* Fostering learning through study groups is a hallmark of a learning community. Study group discussions can be formal or informal, a part of in-class or after-class activities. Sharing information, brainstorming, developing ideas, exploring alternatives, and understanding opposing viewpoints are all outcomes of the cooperative nature of these discussions. Study groups assume that all individuals participating in the discussion have information available to them that could be of help to the other members of the group.

*Peer Tutoring and Peer Teaching.* Even within the same class, students with similar abilities can work with each other in cooperative learning situations. Having students teach new concepts to their peers not only reinforces the concept for the "teacher," but also adds more immediacy and relevance for the "student."

*Peer Evaluation.* Peer evaluation on written and performance work can be an extremely valuable learning tool. Student respondents sharpen their own critical thinking skills and are able to use their experience evaluating others to improve their own work.

## The Role of the Instructor in Cooperative-Learning Communities

It is important to note at this point that the role of the instructor is crucial in creating and maintaining a cooperative-learning community. In the most general terms, it must be understood that *more*, not less, attention must be paid to pedagogy when taking both content and process learning issues into account to promote cooperative-learning communities. Promoting cooperation involves more planning, more attention to individual learning needs, more emphasis on the instructor as a resource person than would be the case in more traditional lecture courses. Class members are accountable to each other for their learning, and the professor is accountable to each one of them. It is that simple and that complex.

Further, the cooperative approach involves a commitment to a longer-term *process* of setting expectations and teaching cooperation skills during the course of the academic term. For one thing, most students arrive with little or no background in cooperation, because they come from secondary schools where competition is the norm. The fundamental rules of a cooperative classroom will be foreign to them, and they must be taught the new set of behaviors to go along with the rules. Cooperative behaviors, in turn, will need to be both reinforced and rewarded.

This means that if competition is the basic mode of operation in the classroom, viable "cooperative assignment" or "cooperation day" or "cooperation week" projects are doomed to fail. Instead of a significant means of promoting student learning, these cooperative models will only serve as a kind of interesting counterpoint to business as usual. It takes time to build the kind of classroom learning community in which students truly are there for each other. First, the cooperative approach must be established as a worthy process, not just as a bag of tricks to resort to when needed.

Finally, it must be understood that when talking about creating a collaborative learning community, that community does not just involve collaboration among students, but between students and faculty as well. The faculty member is a part of the community, contributing and learning with the rest of the class.

### Facilitating Classroom Communities

Several considerations must be taken into account when creating a cooperative-learning community.

*Establishing Relationships.* Students will only choose to be part of a community where they feel comfortable, accepted, and respected. Any instructor who expects truly cooperative learning must allow the students to get to know each other and the instructor in ways that nurture trusting relationships. Students must be drawn into the community of the classroom by sharing appropriate information about themselves and learning about the other members of the community.

*Emphasis on Collaborative Skills.* It is often assumed that a group of students working together will magically produce more work, faster, and it will be of better quality than work they would have produced individually. Perhaps if the entire educational system encouraged cooperative learning, this would be a safe assumption. But the fact is that few of our students are able to transfer the cooperative skills that they have developed interpersonally into academic situations.

Instructors have a responsibility to facilitate learning communities in the classroom by teaching skills related to discussion, feedback, problem solving, agenda setting, delegation, and leadership. Unfortunately, these skills, so essential for cooperative learning, are often taken for granted.

*Time On Task.* Cooperative learning experiences provide significant benefits, but these benefits come at the expense of time, both in class and out of class. Group processes take longer than individual processes. Learning communities can only flourish in situations where the process, which must accompany cooperative learning activities, is allotted ample time.

*Goals of the Instructor.* Unfortunately, many so-called cooperative-learning experiences are thinly disguised activities designed for the purpose of reducing work. What overworked instructor has not toyed with the rationalization that if groups of students write term papers together, then only a few are turned in for evaluation instead of 25 or 30? The motivation for designing a classroom around cooperative learning experiences needs to be examined carefully. For the instructor, setting up a cooperative learning class necessitates *more*, not less, attention to pedagogy.

*Ample Rewards.* Cooperative learning will only be successful if students know they have the opportunity to succeed. This is only possible in an environment that offers unlimited rewards and where students compete against set and understood criteria, instead of against each other. Not every student may receive an "A," but they all could work together if they meet the criteria. Nothing kills the cooperative spirit faster than trying to get students to cooperate when it is clear there are only limited rewards available—only a few students can "win." In response to the perceived problem of "grade inflation," some institutions require grading policies which mandate a particular GPA (for instance a 2.5 class grade average) for undergraduate classes. It is clear why cooperative learning is not part of the culture at these universities.

## Summary

Many misconceptions about cooperative learning are promoted by those who don't understand that competition is not the only way to motivate students. Cooperative learning does not mean eliminating grades, does not mean that the students define the content of the course, and does not mean that essential course content is eliminated in favor of an emphasis on group process. Cooperative learning *does* mean that students are encouraged to learn together and to share their experiences and expertise with their peers.

Cooperative learning experiences are an important part of a student's intellectual and personal growth. Few skills besides the ability to work well with others in a productive manner will have as much impact on an individual's future and career. Because our students have been taught to compete throughout their previous educational experiences, it is up to instructors to facilitate cooperative learning communities in their classrooms—communities where everyone, including the instructor, can "win."

## A Program Built Around Cooperative-Learning Experiences

An emphasis on cooperative learning is one of the hallmarks of the undergraduate nursing program at Winona State University. Students are admitted to the program during the first quarter of their junior year. Each entering cohort proceeds through the two-year sequence of courses together. The creation of a cooperative-learning community among the students and faculty is essential and emphasized throughout the program.

The first class in the nursing sequence, Nurse-Client Interaction, serves a pivotal role in the creation of the learning community. Through emphasis on cooperative skills (communication, self-awareness, values clarification, assertiveness, and group process) in role play and group exercises, students sharpen their cooperative abilities at the same time they begin to create the learning community which will support them academically and interpersonally throughout the following two years.

Two classes in particular epitomize the principle of cooperative learning in action. The junior seminar uses a case study approach designed to simulate a healthcare delivery setting in which a team of people is responsible for the welfare of the patient and the outcomes of nursing care. In this course, students join both a study group and a learning group. Faculty members serve as advisors and consultants. Each study group meets with a faculty consultant to learn about the specific case, identifies what additional information is necessary, locates individuals and organizations from which to obtain the desired information, and prepares a one-hour presentation to the learning group and a paper for the faculty consultant.

The senior seminar in management combines both active

learning and cooperative learning in a hospital setting. Groups of students are assigned to a nursing unit in a local hospital and charged with assessing the learning needs of the staff in that unit. Each group is responsible for developing a learning plan based upon adult learning principles, implementing and evaluating the learning plan, and modifying it for the future.

In these two classes as well as others in the curriculum, peer evaluation plays a significant role. Students evaluate each others' work frequently, often creating the evaluation instruments themselves. Through this practice, they not only learn constructive criticism of others' work, but also can view their own work in the context of the evaluation criteria.

Encouraging cooperative learning can be accomplished many ways—by specific teaching techniques designed to encourage student cooperation, by well-designed projects which require student cooperation, and—in the largest sense—the creation of a cooperative learning community.

## Cooperative Learning: The Principle in Action

There are a number of techniques, used in classrooms across the country, that encourage collaborative learning.

- In a first-year composition course at the University of Minnesota, students leave behind a gift for those students to come: a videotape of themselves discussing their apprehensions before taking the course, their feelings when receiving their papers back, and what they have learned as a result of the class. This tape is shown the following quarter to new students taking the course, usually after their first papers have been returned. The videotape helps students understand that the feelings they are experiencing are shared by others and helps motivate them to succeed, as previous students have in the course.

    Paul Baepler
    Composition and Communication
    University of Minnesota
    Minneapolis, MN 55455
    (612) 626-3000

- The Writing Lab at Massachusetts Bay Community College is a remedial writing program based entirely upon groups for which students provide all materials and curriculum. This program is unusual because it doesn't involve grammar drills, individualized skills work, or tutoring. Instead, its goal is simply for students to make authoritative judgments about their own writing—and whether those judgments correspond with the rules of standard English. Student writers negotiate language choices with their peers, not attempting to second guess "what teachers want."

    Susan Andrien, Writing Coordinator
    Massachusetts Bay Community College
    50 Oakland Street
    Wellesley Hills, MA 02181
    (617) 237-1100

- Students in communication courses at Miami University are encouraged to develop a team "code of conduct" to help facilitate cooperative learning. A sample code is distributed for use as a model. The sample code includes:

    - respect each other
    - criticize ideas instead of people
    - listen actively
    - seek to understand before being understood
    - contribute to group discussion
    - keep an open mind
    - share responsibility
    - attend all meetings

    Students are encouraged to customize the code by adding other shared concerns they might have to the document. Moreover, this becomes a "living" document when they (faculty and/or students) refer to it at the end of each class or group meeting to assess their performance and identify areas for improvement. This works well because it reinforces the philosophy of continuous improvement by encouraging regular assessment based on shared principles and criteria. It also gives license to any group member to point out when the principles are being violated so immediate corrective actions can be implemented.

Gary Shulman
Department of Communication
Miami University
Oxford, OH 45056
(513) 529-7179
e-mail: Shulman_Gary@msmail.muohio.edu

- Students in the Human Rights and Applied Ethics course at Lewis-Clark State College participate in both heterogeneous and homogeneous groupings. Early in the course, students identify the most salient variables for the issues to be discussed in the class. Students are identified and grouped according to the variables, with all students placed into a group with four similar others and into another group with four dissimilar others. The two groups are used throughout the semester, with careful attention paid to which group would be best for the particular topic being discussed. This double grouping helps students both to develop a supportive learning community and to understand diverse ways of thinking.

Rhett Diessner
Lewis-Clark State College
Lewiston, ID 83501
(208) 746-2341

Collaborative testing is being used successfully at many colleges and universities.

- Students in classes at Naugatuck Valley Community-Technical College are tested both individually and within collaborative groups. Although students know when tests will be given, they are unaware of which approach (individual or group) will be used on any given day. Group tests are highly structured, and everyone in the group must agree with the group's answer. This collaborative testing model helps students experience a sensitivity for diversity and others' points of view; develop and refine skills in persuasion, listening, and reading; and share responsibility and accountability. Additionally, students report less test anxiety.

Sharon Shapiro
Naugatuck Valley Community-Technical College
Waterbury, CT 06708
(203) 575-0328

- A form of collaborative test tasking is used at Barry University in Florida. After receiving the essay questions, students are given twenty minutes to consult their notes and discuss the questions with other students. After the twenty-minute exchange, students write their essays, using notes and outlines that they prepared during that time period.

Charles Cassini
Department of Philosophy
Barry University
1130 NE 2nd Ave.
Miami, FL 33161
(305) 899-3000

## Student Projects

- Each semester in Bucknell University's introductory course in organization and management, 150 or so students create and manage companies. Students (typically, 32 to 36 in each company) establish their own service and business missions, design and staff their own organizations, develop control systems (including standards and procedures for performance evaluations), implement projects, and provide a final report to the university community at the end of the semester. These project companies are not "simulations" or "games;" they operate with budgets of $3000 to $5000 each, deliver real services to clients, and develop and sell real products to customers. The course has been widely recognized as an innovative model for active and collaborative pedagogies for undergraduate general education students.

John Miller, Professor of Management
Bucknell University
Lewisburg, PA 17837
(717) 524-1303
e-mail: JMiller@Bucknell.edu

- At the University of St. Thomas, the team-taught course in

"Symbolic Systems: Forms of Visual and Verbal Communication" requires students to work in teams to examine various verbal and visual symbol systems to gain an understanding of the way in which cultural meaning and identity are created. Students study selected readings, advertisements, media, metaphors, and iconology in order to familiarize themselves with existing systems that represent significant aspects of modern culture. Each student group creates a culture and presents it to the class. The project is evaluated on research, ideas, teamwork, and effort. The object of the assignment is to promote synthesis of research, creative thought, and visual ideas.

Lori J. Abrams/Susan Webster
University of St. Thomas
St. Paul, MN 55105
(612) 962-5826
e-mail: LJAbrams@stthomas.edu

• Knox College students have the opportunity to work collaboratively in the publishing of *Catch,* the college's literary magazine. *Catch* demands interaction among the writing students with those in visual arts and photography. In addition to *Catch,* the college provides other opportunities for collaboration in the arts. Written works generate other art activities: plays are produced; poems are put to music. In the process of finding a public outlet for these creative achievements, other campus artists are given the chance to participate in the creative process.

Robin Metz, Director, Program in Writing
Knox College
Galesburg, IL 61401
(309) 343-6746

In some cases, cooperation among students can be dependent upon the learning environment. Flexible classroom space and the use of tables and chairs instead of individual desks can all enhance cooperation among students.

• Umpqua Community College's computer lab for English composition classes features custom-built furniture with four computers per station. This groups students in foursomes which facilitates the cooperative learning methods used by the instructional staff.

Dr. James O'Neill
P.O. Box 967
Umpqua Community College
Roseburg, OR 97470
(503) 440-4625
FAX (503) 440-4666

## Learning Communities

Beyond the creation of student projects, some institutions have student cooperation at the core of their culture. At these institutions, cooperation among students goes beyond group projects and instead is a basic foundation upon which students' education is built.

- A maximum of sixty first-year students at Gustavus Adolphus College—in lieu of fulfilling traditional distribution requirements—may elect to enroll in Curriculum II. Each group of students, along with a team of twelve faculty members from a variety of disciplines, forms a community of learners. The program is designed to instill an appreciation of different ways of knowing and searching for the truth.

    Richard Fuller, Director of Curriculum II
    Gustavus Adolphus College
    800 West College Avenue
    St. Peter, MN 56082
    (507) 933-7311

- At St. John's College in Annapolis, MD, faculty members are called "tutors." Tutors are not allowed to lecture to students. Instead, they are expected to lead discussions, pose questions about the readings, and help guide students toward reaching their own conclusions. As a result, students—not tutors—are each other's primary teachers. Through this process, students learn to cooperate with each other, to take responsibility for their decisions, and learn how to ask questions.

    Geoffrey Comber
    St. John's College
    P.O. Box 2800
    Annapolis, MD 21404
    (410) 263-2371

- Learning communities were developed at Edmonds Community College in order to promote active, engaged collaboration between students. Programs include both coordinated studies and linked courses offered in the humanities, social science, natural science, mathematics, and computing.

  Coordinated Studies Program
  Edmonds Community College
  20000 68th Ave. West
  Lynnwood, WA 98036
  (206) 771-7407

## *Implementing Collaborative Learning*

One powerful way to support the idea of cooperative learning is for faculty to model it among themselves.

- Faculty at the College of Staten Island (CUNY) formed a Collaborative Learning Study Group to share practical ideas on the use of collaborative exercises in their classrooms.

  Peter Miller
  Collaborative Learning Study Group
  Department of English
  College of Staten Island, 2800 Victory Blvd.
  Staten Island, NY 10314
  (718) 982-3670
  FAX (718) 982-3643

- Faculty may find a four-column planning chart is an effective way to integrate collaborative activities into an entire course. The first column identifies a major topic or questions or a fundamental concept, principle, or skill. The second column focuses on a specific learning outcome for the item listed in the first column. The third column identifies the instructional function of the collaborative activity, and the fourth column describes the specific collaborative activity. This systematic method helps instructors use collaborative learning effectively by carefully considering the goal of each activity within the context of the broader learning objective.

Susan Prescott
Department of Education
California State University, Dominquez Hills
Carson, CA 90744
(310) 516-3300

*Tim Hatfield is Professor and Chairperson of the Department of Counselor Education, Winona State University.*

*Susan Rickey Hatfield is Professor and Chairperson of the Department of Communication Studies, Winona State University.*

## References

Tinto, V. (1993). *Building Learning Communities for New College Students: A Summary of Research Findings of the Collaborative Learning Project.* University Park, PA: National Center on Postsecondary Teaching, Learning, and Assessment.

## Resources: Collaborative Learning

The National Center on Postsecondary Teaching, Learning, and Assessment (a federally funded research and development center) has developed a sourcebook on collaborative learning and is in the process of creating a second volume which will consist of a series of strategies that faculty have found to be effective in promoting collaborative learning. Contact: NCTLA, Penn State University, Julie Keehner, 403 S. Allen St. Suite 104, University Park, PA 16801. FAX (814) 865-3638.

Baepler, P. (1993). Electronic one room school house. *The Teaching Professor,* 7 (1), 5.

Cassini, C. (1994). Collaborative testing, grading. *The Teaching Professor,* 8 (4), 5.

Confronting the ethical concerns of corporate life: Bucknell University. (1988). *Liberal Education,* 74 (1), 27–28.

Cooperative Learning and College Teaching. Network for cooperative learning in Higher Education, HFA B316, 100 E. Victoria street, Carson, CA. 90747.

Creative writing leads to other arts: Knox College. (1989). *Liberal Education,* 75 (2), 22–23.

Diessner, R. (1993). Double grouping: New strategies for collaborative learning. *The Teaching Professor,* 7 (9), 1.

Formats for group work. (1994). *The Teaching Professor,* 8 (5), 1–2.

Goodsell, A. S., Maher, M. R., Tinto, V., Smith, B. L. & McGregor. (1992) *Collaborative Learning: A Sourcebook for Higher Education.* (ERIC) Microfiche ED 357 705.

Grading student projects: A project in itself. (1994). Adapted from *For Your Consideration, 3 (3),* by *The Teaching Professor,* 8 (2) , 3–4.

Hansen, E. (Ed.) (1991). Collaborative Learning in Higher Education. Proceedings of the Teaching Conference. Bloomington, Indiana.

Johnson, D. W. & Johnson, R. T. (1985) *Cooperative Learning: Warm Ups, Grouping Strategies and Group Activities.* Edina, MN: Interaction Book Co.

Johnson, D. W. & Johnson, R. T. (1989). *Cooperative and Competition: Theory and Research.* Edina, MN: Interaction Book Co.

Johnson, D. W. & Johnson, R. T. (1991). *Cooperative Learning: Increasing College Faculty Instructional Productivity.* Washington, D. C.: School of Education and Human Development, George Washington University.

Johnson, D. W. & Johnson, R. T. (1989). *Cooperative Learning Lesson Structures.* Edina, MN: Interaction Book Co.

Johnson, D. W., Johnson, R. T., & Holubec, E. J. (1992). *Advanced Cooperative Learning.* Edina, MN: Interaction Book Co.

Johnson, D. W., Johnson, R. T., & Smith, K. A. (1991). *Active Learning: Cooperation in the Classroom.* Edina, MN: Interaction Book Co.

Korshaven, S. Group Projects: Loafing and striving. (1994). *The Teaching Professor,* 8 (4), 4.

McKinney, K. and Graham-Buxton, M. (1993). The use of collaborative learning groups in the large class: Is it possible? *Teaching Sociology,* 21, 403–408.

Prescott, S. (1992). Cooperation and motivation. *Cooperative Learning and College Teaching,* 3 (1).

Reading great books makes good teachers: St. John's College. (1992). *Liberal Education,* 78 (3), 40–41.

Shapiro, S. (1994). Collaborative testing. *The Teaching Professor*, 8 (5), 5.

Shulman, G. & Luechauer, D. (1993) The empowering educator: A CQI approach to classroom leadership. In D. Hubbard (ed.) *Continuous Quality Improvement: Making the Transition to Education* (pp. 424–453). Maryville, MO: Prescott Publishing.

Studying physics within the context of culture: Gustavus Adolphus College. (1988). *Liberal Education, 74* (2), 25–26.

Tinto, V., Goodsell-Love, A., and Russo, P. (1993). Building community. *Liberal Education.* p. 16–21.

# 3

# WHAT IS ACTIVE LEARNING?

*David G. Brown and Curtis W. Ellison*

## Active Learning: An Overview

All educators should spend some time with a one-year-old child whose day revolves around learning. Every new encounter is an adventure; every new idea a revelation. One-year-olds learn through exploration and experimentation. They feel, taste, shake, drop, smell, and examine carefully everything in their world. Once they are familiar with the object, they turn it upside down and explore it all over again. Small children find joy in the process of exploration. They are the quintessential active learners.

What has happened to these active learners by the time they get to our institutions? When did our students stop being excited about the process of learning? When and why did learning cease to be a "hands on" activity?

Whatever happened to university students probably happened long before they came to our institutions. John Goodlad, in his classic *A Place Called School* (1984), bemoaned the mind-numbing, passivity-promoting content acquisition and desk work approach which all too frequently was the norm in his nationwide survey of secondary schools. When faced with the confines of the academic calendar and the large amount of information to be covered in a certain class (see Chapter 5: Time on Task), lecturing becomes an attractive mode of instruction. It is economical in terms of use of course time, it can be planned out in advance, it can be used over and over, and it lets the teacher remain "in control" of the situation. Lectures leave little to chance. Students are moved from concept to concept, idea to idea, sometimes without an understanding of how the information relates to their own lives or the lives of others, or how it has influenced the past, present, or future.

Active learning is not merely a set of activities, but rather an attitude on the part of both students and faculty that makes learning effective. Active learning can best take place in an educational institution which is deliberately shaped to achieve this commitment and when educators are aware that they are responsible for arranging student learning experiences in a developmental way. The objective of active learning is to stimulate lifetime habits of thinking.

There are several levels at which active learning can occur, ranging from a particular approach to completing an assignment in a class to the overall design of a college. The concept of active learning has been applied to curriculum design and to residence life, to internship programs, community service, laboratory science instruction, to musical and speech performance, seminar classes, undergraduate research, peer teaching, computer-assisted learning, and, by some, to engaging lecturers who model aspects of a learning process before large groups. A common element in all these diverse events is that something happens to stimulate students to think about *how* as well as *what* they are learning and to increasingly take responsibility for their own education.

### Encouraging Active Learning

Among the many dimensions of active learning are writing, discussion, peer teaching, research, internships and community experiences. These kinds of active experiences help students understand and integrate new information.

*Writing.* Students need to be encouraged to think about what they are learning and write about it. Journals, application papers, essays, even letters, help students understand by having them articulate their ideas, thoughts, and feelings.

In 1988 Joseph Katz and others published a report for the

Association of American Colleges titled *A New Vitality in General Education*. They viewed active learning as something that teachers must create by asking, "How can the questions our courses raise become our student's own questions?" The Katz group suggested classroom techniques for "stimulating active comprehension" such as asking students to write—during class—their own interpretation of assigned readings or a teacher's presentation, as a way of absorbing a day's work.

*Debate and Discussion.* Debate and discussion, both formal and informal, in class and out of class, help students understand not only theories and concepts but also how these are interpreted and advocated by others. Advocating positions different from their own (role reversal) forces students to examine opposing arguments. When individuals or groups engage in discussion or debate, the result intensifies learning because students are conscientiously teaching others as well as learning from them.

*Peer Teaching.* A key component of the educational experience is students' direct acceptance of responsibility through appropriate, carefully chosen role-taking, often involving human helping of some kind. This can take many forms, including peer helping, cross-age teaching, mentoring of younger students, or tutoring. Studying laboratory science by a discovery-oriented method—where student groups work with faculty to design and conduct basic experiments, then replicate the results by teaching the experiment to other student groups—has a strong active-learning as well as cooperative-learning aspect.

*Research.* The opportunity to design, discover, explore, and execute creates powerful learning experiences. Students need to learn, first-hand, how to manipulate conditions and variables and both predict and observe the results of these manipulations.

In addition to conducting research on their own, the opportunity to work with other students and with faculty on research projects promotes cooperative learning and student-faculty interaction.

*Practice.* Students need to have the opportunity to practice what they have learned, in both real and hypothetical situations. Case studies give students such an opportunity and allow them to apply their critical thinking skills. Ideally, this kind of learning practice should be supervised or mentored to give students assistance and feedback to help them improve.

## Summary

To achieve an active learning environment requires a change on the part of both students and faculty. Students need to come into a college or university with an attitude of becoming an active part of the intellectual community of that institution. Faculty need to examine their assumptions about learning to create active-learning communities in their classes, their disciplines, and their institutions.

In some circumstances, faculty commitment to active learning may influence the overall design of a degree-granting program, a small college, or a school within a university. In these cases educators are seeking to design an institution so that teaching and learning, often in concert with faculty research, are at the center of everyone's attention. The following illustration shows the kinds of active learning that may be engaged in by students moving through a four-year core curriculum linked to a career development program and a personalized focus of study.

## A Residential College Devoted to Active Learning

Miami University's School of Interdisciplinary Studies, Western College Program, is a residential college within a state university. Active learning in the Western Program is regarded as evolutionary for both students and professors. At the summer orientation program, before the first year begins, new students (and their parents) are asked to write out their expectations for the coming semester. This exercise encourages self-awareness about expectations.

The core curriculum for the students' first year requires courses in natural science, social science, humanities and arts designed and taught by full-time faculty working in teams. Courses are organized to integrate various fields of study, and annual community learning themes encourage intellectual discussions outside classes. Themes of "community," "gender," and "diversity" have stimulated considerable debate and initiated students effectively into the program's active learning agenda. A fourth required course in the first year treating fine arts and technology in consecutive terms is designed by faculty deliberately to take students beyond the text-based instruction associated with lecture and seminar learning in their other core courses. In this fourth course, students may learn idea formation in nonverbal ways through elementary design exercises. They may study community interactions by recreating ritual events or conduct discovery-oriented laboratory or field experiments that deepen understandings of the impact of technology in daily life. Interactive video-disk projects and distance learning in the program's computer-assisted learning laboratory are possible.

For the second year of the core curriculum, faculty teams design courses that deliberately combine broad fields of inquiry. All courses in the second year involve such things as group projects, projects initiated by students that are related to course themes, and work with original sources through ethnographic analysis, oral history research, or community projects.

In each year of the curriculum, students must write extensively. They are actively involved in the learning process by in-class writing that builds comprehension, by keeping reflective journals and by laboratory reports, bibliographic papers, short analytical studies, creative writing projects, research papers, and reports.

Instead of pursuing majors designed by a faculty committee, students in the Western Program work with faculty advisors and program administrators to write formal learning contracts that govern their advanced studies. The "Statement of Educational Objectives" is both an advising device and a means for engaging students in thoughtful career planning as early as their sophomore year. A junior-year internship, field study, or arrangement for study abroad is encouraged and may be included in the student's focus. Writing the learning contract in the sophomore year and revising it thereafter helps students take ownership of the curriculum they are pursuing, increases motivation, and builds a sense of personal responsibility for their education—key features of active learning.

In the final year, students complete a self-initiated, year-long senior project. This extensive work is carried out with an assigned faculty advisor and with the support of a senior project workshop. The workshop meets weekly to share research developments and discuss project design, execution, and progress. A senior project conference in a professional-meeting format is held in late spring.

Here students share results of their projects in panel discussions and hear faculty critics from throughout the university and elsewhere. The quality of this event suggests the overall quality of academic learning in the Western Program as well as the effectiveness of student initiative and understanding. It is also an important symbolic closing of the college years.

## Active Learning: The Principle In Action

Across the country, innovations aimed at developing student responsibility for learning can be viewed as indicators of institutional and educational distinction. Examples of the good practice of active learning range from engaging students in the learning process through the encouragement of writing and discussion, to students actively participating in research and student-created organizations.

### *Encouraging Faculty to Implement Active Learning*

Faculty generally agree on the merits of active learning. Unfortunately, changing from a "business as usual" approach to one that promotes active learning requires a fundamental rethinking of classroom structure and policies. Incentives from both internal and external sources might help facilitate this change.

• Northeast Missouri State University has received a substantial private donation to support active learning initiatives. The Jepson Fellowships (named for the donors) support faculty in the research and development of active learning strategies as well as dissemination of results on campus. The intent of the fellowships is to recognize the broadest possible interpretation of active learning in an effort to stimulate innovative teaching and learning experiences.

> Office of the Vice President for Academic Affairs
> Northeast Missouri State University
> Kirksville, MO 63501
> (816) 785-4000

### *Involving Students in the Learning Process*

Programs and individual courses at many institutions emphasize approaches to learning designed to actively engage students.

- At Iowa State University, history students govern the classroom as they interview prominent individuals during a press conference, such as George Washington as he retired from his post as Commander-in-Chief of the Continental Army or Lord George Grenville about reasons for the Stamp Act. After the press conferences, students work in groups identifying the main ideas and creating headlines and news articles that highlight those ideas.

  Clair Keller
  Department of History
  Iowa State University
  Ames, IA 50011
  (515) 294-7266

- An education professor at the University of Wisconsin-LaCrosse has created a hypothetical school system (complete with administration, teachers, pupils, and families) to help his students learn about the legal intricacies of special education. Throughout the semester, students play the roles of parents, teachers, administrators, lawyers, and students as they participate in complex legal cases involving students with disabilities. Not only do students develop an understanding of the human side of these cases, they also gain an understanding of the law as it applies to special education and students with disabilities.

  Stuart Robertshaw
  Department of Education
  University of Wisconsin
  LaCrosse, WI 54601
  (608) 785-8000

- To help promote active discussion in his classroom, a faculty member at the University of Southern Indiana includes a set of discussion guidelines in the course syllabus. The guidelines include:

  - Try to connect ideas from the course with phenomena outside the classroom, and between ideas in one part of the course and those in a different part

  - Value tentativeness. It's OK to admit you're unsure

  - Try to avoid war stories, rambling speeches heavily punctuated with the pronoun "I"

Howard Gabennesch
Sociology Department
University of Southern Indiana
Evansville, IN 47712
(812) 464-8600

- At the United States Air Force Academy, war gaming is incorporated into history courses by the use of popular board games and computer simulation. Upon completion of the "game," students write a comparison of the results of their game to the historical situation.

Lt. Col. Bill Williams
Dept. Of History
HQ USAFA/DFH
USAF Academy, CO 80840
(719) 472-3230
FAX (719) 472-2970
e-mail: WilliamsWJ%DFH@dfmail.usafa.af.mil

- In an organizational behavior class, students are given several small packets of assessment instruments during the semester to complete and score at home (e.g. personality attributes, decision making style, ways they handle conflict, etc.). Each packet is related to the next topic in class. Students anonymously report their scores on the various instruments. Data from the class is compiled and discussed in comparison to national norms. For each instrument the teacher begins a discussion of the implementation of being at, above, or below the norm, things to watch out for, and practical ways and approaches to try to strengthen each area. Students are encouraged to ask questions about the meaning of the instrument's score. Not only do students learn about themselves, but they get practice in compiling and reporting data and they get exposure to statistical concepts in a non-threatening way.

Len Tischler, Ph.D.
School of Management
University of Scranton
Scranton, PA 18510
(717) 941-7782

- Students in the organizational communication class at Miami University and the organizational behavior class at Butler University get to experience what they are being taught about empowering work environments as faculty incorporate the principles of organizational development into their classes. In an effort to forge an open, creative team environment, students help design the syllabus, generate class requirements, identify criteria for measuring participation, and design the final project. Student feedback identifies increased feelings of ownership, self-efficacy, and motivation as the benefits of this approach.

  Gary Shulman
  Department of Communication
  Miami University
  Oxford, OH 45056
  (513) 529-7179
  e-mail: Shulman_Gary@msmail.muohio.edu

- Every four years, half a dozen Wake Forest University students take about $30,000 of student fee money to New York City. Their mission is to purchase more art for the Student Union. In preparation for the journey, the decision-making students enroll in a semester course where strategies of art collection are studied.

  Harry Titus, Associate Professor
  Department of Art
  Wake Forest University
  P.O. Box 7232
  Reynolds Station
  Winston-Salem, NC 27109
  (910) 759-5081

- Structured journal writing is a major part of several classes at Lesley College, including courses offered in developmental English, biology, music, math, psychology, and education. Each journal entry has two parts: the first paragraph emphasizes points for recall and retention; the second part emphasizes application of the content to the student's life experience and observation.

Donna Cole, Director of the Writing Center
Lesley College
29 Everett Street
Cambridge, MA 02138
(617) 349-8460

This "hands on" approach—especially in the sciences—has been found to be particularly effective with students new to higher education, either as traditional first-year students or students returning to the classroom after a several-year absence. In addition, an active learning approach has also been found to be effective in reaching students new to a particular field of study.

- Non-science majors taking "Discovery, Innovation, and Risk" at the Claremont Colleges in California buy a few strips of balsa wood, some string, and a little glue. Their assignment is to create the lightest, least expensive, and most elegant bridge that will span 75 centimeters and hold 20 kilograms. The project is one of the ways in which hands-on experience is provided in a two-semester sequence that blends technological applications with the principles of the natural sciences.

Newton Copp, Professor of Biology
Andrew Zanella, Professor of Chemistry
The Joint Science Department
The Claremont Colleges
925 North Mills Avenue
Claremont, CA 91711
(714) 621-8298
e-mail: copp@jsd.claremont.edu

- Students at Iona College learn the laws of physics, the description of electrical currents, the creation and behavior of sound waves, and the role of magnetism through the writing and playing of music on computers.

Victor Stanionis, STL Curriculum Director
Department of Physics
Iona College
New Rochelle, NY 10801
(914) 633-2236
FAX (914) 633-2240

- Several departments at Dickinson College have adopted a "workshop" approach to teaching introductory-level science courses. Instead of traditional lecture/lab courses, students in physics, chemistry, and mathematics participate in classes that emphasize hands-on experimentation and encourage peer discussion. The Physics Department is revising its curriculum to appeal to students with broader interests than pure physics, and to incorporate more project-centered courses. Students majoring in physics progress from the workshop introductory course through intermediate and advanced courses to a research experience at the senior level.

Priscilla Laws, Professor and Chair Department of Physics
Dickinson College
Carlisle, PA 17013
(717) 245-1599
e-mail: Laws@dickinson.edu

## *Student Research*

A number of institutions offer opportunities for student research. In addition to offering research opportunities, the University of North Carolina at Asheville also offers outlets for students to share their research.

- At the University of North Carolina at Asheville, students partner with faculty in scholarly research. This visible emphasis of the university is supported by grants to students and features a national journal of student writing as well as a national conference on undergraduate research. Tutorial relationships with faculty and field experiences are an important part of the research program. Talented students receive four-year scholarships and undergraduate teaching awards. The goals of this program are to expand the student's self-confidence and knowledge and to make meaningful contributions in the student's chosen field.

John Stevens, Professor
Department of Chemistry
University of North Carolina-Asheville
One University Heights
Asheville, NC 28804
(704) 251-6617

Active learning through experimentation can be powerfully enhanced when combined with another form of active learning— role play—which allows for explorations of important issues related to the question.

- Alternating laboratory experiments with seminars on ethical and social issues is one feature of the Science and Technological Literacy (STL) courses at Iona College. For instance, students used a cartridge filter to simulate the effects of a kidney transplant machine then participated in role play, as family members, physician, and hospital administrator, to decide whether a homeless alcoholic should have a kidney transplant.

Victor Stanionis, STL Curriculum Director
Department of Physics
Iona College
New Rochelle, NY, 10801
(914) 633-2236, FAX (914) 633-2240

### *Student Projects*
Student-created and -operated organizations and projects encourage both active learning and cooperation among students.

- At Miami University, students majoring in marketing, telecommunication, and graphic arts are given the opportunity to participate in Laws Hall and Associates. Laws Hall students form three advertising agencies that plan, write, and produce all media for a full advertising campaign. The client, usually a major corporation introducing a new product, orients all teams to their needs and judges the final products. The multi-disciplinary course is taught by faculty from three departments and involves about 100 students. Each of the student advertising agencies is organized with the officers and professionals typical of a "real world" agency.

William L. Utter, Director
Laws Hall and Associates
Miami University
Oxford, OH 45056
(513) 529-3532

- The Math Clinic Program at Harvey Mudd College offers students an opportunity to develop the modeling and analysis tools necessary to solve applied problems under conditions closely approximating an industrial setting. Problems originate from a variety of sources: industry, business, government. The Clinic requires teamwork to complete each project.

> Robert Borrelli, Chairperson
> The Math Clinic
> Harvey Mudd College
> Claremont, CA 91711
> (909) 621-8896

- Teams of Biomedical Engineering seniors at Rensselaer Polytechnic Institute were challenged by the Cerebral Palsy Center to design and build mechanical and electrical devices which would help children at the CP Center lead more independent lives.

> Dr. John Brunski, Dr. Jonathan Newell
> Department of Biomedical Engineering
> Jonsson Engineering Center, Room 7049
> Rensselaer Polytechnic Institute
> Troy, NY 12180-3590
> (518) 276-6547

## Active Learning Outside the College or University

In addition to actively engaging students in on-campus learning opportunities, virtually every college or university offers opportunities for off-campus learning through volunteer activities, field study, internship, or study abroad programs.

- Students enrolled in "Volunteerism and Community Organization" at Temple University know that they are going to spend more time out of class than in it. The only prerequisite for the course is a willingness to spend an hour and a half in class and ten hours per week working at a volunteer organization. Each student keeps a journal documenting the work and presents to the class a summary of the experience. Students gain a broad understanding of how individual and social change occurs as a result of this intense volunteer experience.

> Ronnie Steinberg, Dept. of Sociology

Temple University
Philadelphia, PA 19122
(215) 204-7760

- Students in the School for Social Ecology program at California State University at Irvine focus on the problem-solving aspect of this major through participation in the field study component. This participation is required during a student's junior or senior year and involves about ten hours of work per week for a minimum of one quarter. Students work on a voluntary basis in police departments, legal services offices, child-care facilities, hospitals, pollution-control agencies, and private firms among many others.

Associate Dean for Undergraduate Studies,
School for Social Ecology
University of California-Irvine
Irvine, CA 92717
(714) 856-6094

- Fourteen of Miami University's best students are engaged in full-time internships in businesses and community organizations in Ohio cities. The goals of the program are to foster the students' personal and professional development and to engage their interest in urban issues. To prepare for their internships, the students participate in a seminar which includes an immersion weekend in Dayton where the scope and complexity of city problems come to life in interviews with community leaders. Summer discussions with fellow interns and written journal assignments further support the learning experience.

Francis M. Anderson, Coordinator
5 Harrison Hall
Miami University
Oxford, OH 45056
(513) 529-5643

*David G. Brown is Provost, Wake Forest University, and former Chancellor, University of North Carolina-Asheville.*

*Curtis W. Ellison is Dean of Interdisciplinary Studies, Miami University in Oxford, Ohio.*

## Resources: Active Learning

Cerbin, W. (1993). Fostering a culture of teaching as scholarship. *The Teaching Professor,* 7 (3), 1.

Cummins, H., and Myers, C. (1992). Incorporating sciences in a liberal arts education. *The National Honors Report,* 13 (2).

Gabennesch, H. (1992). Creating quality class discussion. *The Teaching Professor,* 6 (9), 5.

Goodlad, J. I. (1984). *A Place Called School.* New York, NY: McGraw-Hill.

Hands on experience in course's focus: Temple University. (1989). *Liberal Education,* 75 (4), 33–34.

Harrison-Pepper, S. (1991). Dramas of persuasion: Utilizing performance in the classroom. *Journal of Excellence in College Teaching,* 2.

Interdisciplinary approach to technology. (1988). *Liberal Education,* 74, (2), 23–24.

Katz, J., Bornholt, L., Gaff, J.G., Hoffman, N., Newman, L.F., Ratner, M., and Weingartner, R.H. (1968). *A New Vitality in General Education: Task Group on General Education.* Washington, DC: Association of American Colleges.

Lutzker, M. (1988). *Research Projects for College Students.* New York, NY: Greenwood Press.

Nalcolmson, P., and Myers, R. (1993). Debates: Techniques for improving student thinking. *The Teaching Professor,* 7 (3), 6.

New approach to social sciences integrates disciplinary learning: University of California at Irvine. (1990). *Liberal Education,* 76 (2), 23–25.

Shulman, G. & Bernheim, M. (1994). Making business meetings work. In R. Hudson, & B. Selzler (eds.) *Business Communication: Concepts and Applications in an Electronic Age.* (5th ed.) Los Angeles, CA: Roxbury Publishing Company. 33–38.

Studying physics in depth: Dickinson College. (1990). *Liberal Education,* 76 (4), 38–40.

Values examined in science and technology course: Iona College. (1988). *Liberal Education,* 74 (2), 27–28.

**Principle 4: Good Practice Gives Prompt Feedback**

*Knowing what you know and don't know focuses learning. Students need appropriate feedback on performance to benefit from courses. In getting started, students need help in assessing existing knowledge and competence. In classes, students need frequent opportunities to perform and receive suggestions for improvement. At various points during college, and at the end, students need chances to reflect on what they have learned, what they still need to know, and how to assess themselves.*

4

# PROMPT FEEDBACK

*David Benson, Lu Mattson, and Les Adler*

## Prompt Feedback: An Overview

The concept of feedback is a simple yet powerful principle to help guide the learning process. It can be understood at the level of highly sophisticated research or at a more common sense level, with obvious applications for teachers and learners.

This chapter defines feedback as any procedure used to inform a learner of the degree of appropriateness or correctness of a response to an instructional stimulus. The feedback can be oral, written, computer displayed, or any of the more complex interactions that occur in group learning. What is crucial to the definition is that the learner is informed and can associate the feedback with a particular or specific response.

To understand the basic concept of feedback, it is worthwhile to use examples from some of the earliest research done on the topic. To determine the effect of feedback, research subjects were asked to draw a line of a designated length while blindfolded.

With repeated practice the subject was able to draw a line of fairly consistent length; however, the length of the line was usually very different from the length requested. Obviously, if the subject was told the line was too long, the next attempt was likely to be closer to the specified target. Without some type of feedback, improvement in performance did not occur since the subject had no basis for knowing which adjustments to make. Similar research has been done with gunners using heavy artillery. With various forms of information provided as feedback, the learning of accurate aiming was significantly improved.

The importance of feedback is so obvious that it is often taken for granted during the teaching and learning process. When that happens, the full potential associated with appropriate feedback may be lost. For example, we know that students want to have test papers or other projects returned "on time," but what does that mean? Is it better to receive the feedback immediately, the next day, the next week, or does it make any difference? And what about the nature of that feedback? Should it be brief and summative, such as a letter grade, or would a more comprehensive written response be more productive in the learning process?

It is important to understand some of the underlying principles associated with the good practice of prompt feedback. This essay will address the issues of timeliness, directiveness, specificity, amount, and sources of feedback.

### Timeliness of Feedback

Prompt feedback is generally better than postponed feedback. Some delay may be effective in certain circumstances; for instance, some "distancing" of the learner from the details of a lesson may allow a larger conceptualization of the field to occur. In general, however, learning relies on feedback being available at the moment of choice, when a learner needs to select among alternatives, one being preferable to the others. It is this "need to know" which dictates the prompt return of tests at the next class meeting before new material is introduced. Timeliness of feedback leads to effective class interaction, discussion, and question/answer periods.

### Directiveness of Feedback

Feedback is, by definition, directive. When a student is headed toward the correct solution of a problem, acknowledging the correctness of the choices made moves the student forward. For example, noting a clever, well-directed step in an argument or a well-selected example encourages students to believe that they are on a right track. Pointing out that an example is not appropriate or that a step has been missed in the argument warns students to pull back, rethink, reassess.

### Specificity of Feedback

Good practice in this regard lets students know not only whether they are on a right track, but why the answer is a good one or what is keeping it from being so. In other words, "right" and "wrong," "yes" and "no" are less helpful to the student than those assessments accompanied by explanation of what earned the judgment. Generalized feedback is of little value. Simply saying, "That isn't right, try it again" isn't helpful without the offering of suggestions to improve performance.

Often wrong responses are due to lack of understanding of what is needed to correct an incorrect move. For example, "No, that throw is off to the left" tells a young person learning to throw a ball what they already know, but not how to fix it. "Next time, try stepping toward the plate" provides the missing information. Clear expectations can help students in their initial attempts and also can help faculty provide specific feedback.

### Amount of Feedback

Excessive feedback can be counterproductive to learning; inadequate feedback can be also. The right amount is that which allows the learner to grasp the nature of the error and suggests an alteration in response. The student defeated by an over-corrected essay, in which all errors are noted, may see none of them. Noting a pattern of errors and letting the others go for the moment may allow the student to focus on the most important error that could otherwise be lost in the blur of excessive correction. At the other extreme, the same paper simply marked "C-" with little analysis of what might be changed leaves the student guessing. "In that tennis stroke you didn't shift your weight, your elbow was straight, and your grip was too far over on top; now, try it again" is too much to process. "Let's get your thumb back over where it belongs and then shift your weight into the ball" may be about right. "That tree shouldn't be in your painting" is uselessly vague.

"The tree is out of perspective to the rest of the painting; maybe it should be smaller and over to the left" is not.

## Sources of Feedback

Feedback can be provided by many sources, including students and computers, in addition to faculty. By having students provide feedback on each others' work, students sharpen their own critical thinking skills, as well as their ability to articulate feedback in an appropriate manner. Providing feedback to others also allows students a chance to reevaluate their own work after having experienced the work of others. To be successful, students providing feedback need experience in critical thinking and a clear understanding of the evaluation criteria. Having the instructor explain the criteria and expectations is essential. Once students know what they are looking for, evaluating an example (created for this purpose) through group discussion and offering suggestions for improvement is a good way for students to start understanding how to evaluate another's work. It is vital that the instructor take an active role in this exercise, making sure that the evaluations and suggestions are both valid and fair.

In addition to students providing feedback to other students, they need to be encouraged to assess their own work. Rather than the instructor always providing feedback, students need to be asked what they think of their own work. Beyond merely proofreading their papers, students must articulate their perceptions of their performance and be given the opportunity to outline their own goals for improvement. In many cases, these critical evaluations may prove a more important learning experience than the actual paper.

## Summary

Feedback regarding the correctness of a response is essential to the learning process. To be most helpful, feedback normally should be prompt, indicate the direction of change desired, be specific to the particular circumstances, and be given in a quantity that can be understood and acted upon by the learner.

Feedback turns out to be a surprisingly complex element in education. Feedback never really stops; it passes between student and student, student and faculty, faculty and faculty as a web of communication about the growth that is occurring in the individual. It is a vital part of checking to be sure that students are developing an array of information, skills, and techniques that will enable them to learn independently throughout life.

## Feedback in the Hutchins School of Liberal Studies

The Hutchins School of Liberal Studies, one of the academic units within Sonoma State University, is an interdisciplinary, seminar-based program which provides an integrative general education in the lower division and a general liberal-studies major in the upper division. Feedback at Hutchins is a multi-dimensional process involving a variety of measures and including faculty and students in a two-way relationship. Written work is evaluated, graded, and commented upon by the instructor, and by other students as well when it occurs in a tutorial setting.

The Hutchins pedagogy only works if feedback to the participants comes consistently and "on the spot" when special needs arise. But the relationship of seminar to feedback is closer than that: the seminar itself is a feedback mechanism; a student offers an idea about some aspect of a reading, and the other students are there to think about that idea, then build on it or offer what seem to be improvements. Thinking critically implies judgment and the weighing of competing ideas, and in a seminar that happens with assists from one's colleagues. Seminars also include receiving feedback on the spot about the impact of one's ideas on others.

The same close relationship between pedagogy and feedback is present in writing tutorials—which are, in effect, editing workshops. In them, a student circulates copies of a paper that he or she believes to be "finished," and the group goes to work identifying those aspects of the paper that help or interfere with effective communication. The instructor helps by steering the group's attention to points it may have missed and by clarifying technical matters. All of the students are involved directly in a feedback process, either by providing or receiving it.

In fact, the final version of a paper is usually not re-submitted to the group but to the instructor. This process suggests that feedback about writing is helpful before the final product has been achieved, at a point at which the writer can make use of it and not simply endure it (as is the case when only a finished version is evaluated). Aside from what may be said about an individual paper, it is also not unusual for the tutorial group to begin to notice and remark on how a student's later papers may be improving over earlier efforts.

In the seminar and the writing tutorial, it is hard to say who profits more: the individual whose ideas are being evaluated or the individuals offering the feedback. It turns out that in these settings, feedback is a reciprocal process in which the person offering feedback is learning about clarity of thought and expression, the forceful presentation of ideas, and so forth. In these situations, feedback is timely if it is immediate, honest, and relevant.

## Good Feedback Assumes Many Forms: The Principle in Action

Obviously, good feedback practices can be found at many institutions and in many forms. It can occur within an individual classroom or a program or an institution, but it does not occur by chance. Where feedback is thoughtfully carried out, it signals that students are seen as active participants in their own growth; that the educational process at that institution tries to provide the student with cues that are clear, frequent, and timely; and that there is a concern to know that the message, whatever it is, has gotten through.

### Feedback on Exams

There is truth in the idea that to be useful, feedback must be prompt, especially where papers and exam results are concerned. Promptness assumes many forms, all aimed at returning information about performance to a student as soon as possible so that a readjustment of what has been learned can occur if students are confused. Prompt feedback might be mandated by the institution with specific deadlines by which student materials must be returned. More often than not, prompt feedback is the responsibility of the instructor. Simple actions, such as having a copy of the answers to an exam available to students immediately after they have taken a test or scheduling an extra session the day of the exam to explain the correct answers are both methods of providing prompt feedback to students.

Essentially, students' primary concern is how they performed on a particular exam or assignment. After that basic piece of information, they can begin to look at what they have learned. Reinforcement of what they have learned correctly and clarification of what has confused them is linked to the speed with which they can have the materials returned to them.

- At the University of Scranton, a management professor struggled with the timing of tests and quizzes in a 2-3 hour class. Because students are "psyched" for the test, little other learning was occurring during that time block, whether the exam was given at the beginning or end of class. The solution: computer scored multiple choice tests and quizzes which allowed the professor to have the tests scored during the 15 minute class break following the test or quiz. The tests or quizzes are returned immediately after the break, allowing for a class discussion of the exam, question by question. Many students report that they finally understood the material from listening to or participating in the feedback discussion.

Len Tischler, Ph.D.
School of Management
University of Scranton
Scranton, PA 18510
(717) 941-7782

## *Feedback on Writing*

Feedback about writing is especially important. It can range from help from one's peers and structured faculty responses regarding formal writing to interactive journal writing shared by student writer and faculty responder.

- At Hollins College, each student in the Critical Thinking course submits two copies of their papers. The second copy is given to another student who prepares a critique.

Allie Frazier
Department of Philosophy
Hollins College,
Hollins College, VA 24020
(703) 362-6000

Person-to-person feedback occurs at a number of institutions—Northeast Missouri, St. Mary's Maryland, and Fort Lewis College, Co. among them—where journals are a normal part of the student's writing experience. Journals can be used to ascertain what the student is learning, as they are at St. Mary's, or they can be the occasion for dialogue with the student. These "interactive journals" let the faculty member respond on a non-technical, non-judgmental level to the student, a familiar, time-honored feedback element in many programs.

• Feedback is provided back to the instructor throughout the course at Metropolitan State College of Denver where a faculty member circulates a class journal in a spiral notebook during class and invites students to offer constructive feedback on the course. The instructor reads the notebook each evening, and responds to student comments in the journal. The immediate feedback allows the instructor to shape the class to meet student needs, correct misconceptions, and demonstrate that because of student diversity, not all of the students can be pleased all of the time.

> Leslie Swetnam
> Teacher Education Department
> Metropolitan State College of Denver
> 1006 11th Street
> Denver, CO 80204
> (303) 556-6228

## Feedback Using Computers

The use of computers can facilitate timely and complete feedback, as well as allow students and faculty the opportunity to provide feedback to each other in a non-threatening form.

• Faculty in the Communication Studies Department at Winona State University teach multiple sections of the basic course in public speaking each quarter. Faced with the need to evaluate as many as 30 speeches a day and provide complete, prompt feedback, faculty are in the process of creating a set of the most frequent comments on speeches. These comments are coded into a computer program. Speech faculty, using lap top computers, can listen to a speech in class and simply type in the codes of the appropriate comments. This allows faculty to spend time on comments specific to the individual speech, while also providing students with complete and prompt feedback on their entire speech.

Communication Studies Department
Winona State University
Winona, MN 55987
(507) 457-5230
e-mail: CMSTDEPT@Vax2.Winona.MSUS.edu.

## Computer Assisted Instruction

The use of computers for feedback provides faculty with an extra opportunity to offer guidance, as Computer Assisted Instruction (CAI) for coursework begins to come into its own. The computer's instant feedback is a prominent advantage in a well-designed CAI package. Whatever problems there are with developing thoughtful, efficient computer courseware, feedback is not necessarily one of them. Instantaneous feedback for each student "move" makes the computer a potentially powerful teaching tool. Besides, it is generally acknowledged that CAI can allow the student to take risks that would be avoided in the presence of a real-life instructor, since being "wrong" with a computer is not the same thing as being "wrong" with a faculty member. Furthermore, the endless patience of the machine lets the student determine the pace at which instruction will move. The age of widely applicable, truly effective courseware finally seems about to dawn. Some institutions are already putting what there is to good use.

• The University of Illinois reports several instances in which CAI enhances classroom instruction: interactive videodisk technology supports instruction in a chemistry course; computer simulations give students immediate feedback in decision-making exercises; Hypercard stacks provide enrichment as well as immediate feedback in a range of courses from History of Western Thought to Introductory Agricultural Economics.

Lynelle Lucey
University of Illinois
Urbana, IL 61801
(217) 244-1257

• Students in the Introductory Logic course at Winona State University reinforce their classroom learning through the use of an interactive computer program created by Philosophy Department faculty. The program allows students to initiate homework and exam sessions at their own pace. It offers detailed explanations of incorrect answers on homework, as well as reviews of missed problems on exams.

Craig Hansen and Kevin Possin
Department of Philosophy
Winona State University
Winona, MN 55987
(507) 457-5475
e-mail: CHansen@Vax2.Winona.MSUS.edu

## Feedback and Students at Risk

An acknowledgment of the importance of feedback to special groups of "high risk" students underlies the good practices of several other institutions. Among these special groups are weak students, the young, and the underrepresented.

• Southern Utah University has committed itself to creating an environment where only a student who has no desire to learn will fail. Low numbers of students per class assure that faculty will have an opportunity to get to know each student well, and an effort is made to enhance the student's self-image and desire for success. Faculty know how individual students are doing and counsel students who have been absent from class.

Advising Center
Southern Utah University
Cedar City, UT 84720
(801) 586-7700

• North Carolina State University moves the early warning system up in the process so that it occurs one-third of the way through the term for both freshman and transfer students. Courses serving mainly "high risk" students have been identified, and pre-tests provide feedback to the students in those subjects to help them prepare well and therefore do well.

Office of Advising
North Carolina State University
Raleigh, NC 27695
(919) 515-2011

Many institutions get to know their students because they provide residential programs or because they feature active learning.

Some of them have been mentioned or described here. There is, however, another kind of program which offers help to the high-risk student.

- The University of Michigan-Flint offers the Challenge Program, which identifies students from underrepresented groups and provides them with special assistance in developing skills while affording a home base in the institution. Student Service staff and Arts and Humanities faculty cooperate in offering special tutorial services, customized advising, monitoring of progress and personal counseling for these minority and first generation college students. The result has been a higher college grade point average for this group than for the students at large.

    Advising Center
    University of Michigan-Flint
    Flint, MI 48502
    (313) 762-3300

## Feedback from Outside the University

Feedback from individuals outside the university can be valuable to both students and universities by providing a "real world" view to academic accomplishments and programs.

- External assessments are an important part of Alverno College's programs. Corporation managers, teachers, nurses, and other professionals are trained to use Alverno's assessment instruments and serve as volunteer assessors in certain situations.

    Kathleen O'Brien, Academic Dean
    Alverno College
    3401 South 39th Street
    Box 343922
    Milwaukee, WI 53234-3922
    (414) 382-6084

- Penn State's Center for Student Involvement and Leadership surveyed recruiters from various companies. Recruiters cited a lack of leadership and communication skills as problems among beginning engineers. As a result of this survey, Pennsylvania State University then created Project WISE: Workplace Integration Skills for Engineers.

Nancy Narcum
Student Organization Resource Center
Pennsylvania State University
University Park, PA 16802
(814) 863-4624

*David Benson is President Emeritus, Sonoma State University.*

*Lu Mattson is Professor Emeritus, Hutchins School of Liberal Studies, Sonoma State University.*

*Les Adler is Provost, Hutchins School of Liberal Studies, Sonoma State University.*

## Resources: Prompt Feedback

Brinko, K, T. (1993). The practice of giving feedback to improve teaching. *Journal of Higher Education, 64* (5), 574–593.

Clark, K. (1993). Facilitating learning through journals. *Ohio Association of Two Year Colleges' Journal,* 32–34.

Creating a learning community within the philosophy major: Hollins College. (1990). *Liberal Education, 76* (2), 18–20.

Dohrer, G. (1991). Do teachers comments on students' papers help? *College Teaching, 39* (2), 48–54.

Emphasizing what students can do with what they know: Alverno College. (1988). *Liberal Education, 74* (3), 27–29.

Engineering students get WISE to real world skills: Pennsylvania State University. (1990). *Liberal Education, 76* (3), 36–38.

Enhancing instructor-class communication. (1994). *The Teaching Professor,* 8 (3), 3–4.

Liberal arts majors prepare for management positions. (1989). *Liberal Education, 75* (3), 37–39.

More on student self-assessment. (1992). *The Teaching Professor,* 6 (10), 7.

Svinicki, M. D. Four R's of effective evaluation. (1993). Reprinted from The Center for Teaching Effectiveness Newsletter at the University of Texas at Austin, in *The Teaching Professor,* 7 (9), 3–4.

**Principle 5: Good Practice
Emphasizes Time on Task**

*Time plus energy equals learning. Efficient time-management skills are critical for students and professionals alike. Allocating realistic amounts of time means effective learning for students and effective teaching for faculty. How an institution defines time expectations for students, faculty, administrators, and other professional staff can establish the basis for high performance for all.*

5

# TIME ON TASK

*Stuart Vorkink*

## Time on Task: An Overview

It's easy to assume that students would be more successful if they just spent more time studying. While this statement makes intuitive sense, it oversimplifies the principle of time on task. Student achievement is not simply a matter of the amount of time devoted to the task. Although learning and development require time, it is an error to ignore *how much* time is available and *how well* the time is spent.

Time on task is more complex than one might assume. On the surface, it appears this principle is merely a call for teaching our students time management techniques and study skills. But by definition, time on task also involves how the university defines the time available for learning. Faculty members work within the time frame provided by the university to optimize learning through the management of their own instructional time.

### University Use of Time

According to Keith Geiger, President of the National Education Association, "For many decades, the clock has controlled learning. Time has been the constant and learning the variable. If learning is to improve, that dictum must be reversed. Learning must become the constant and time the variable." These comments, though directed at K–12 education, are equally applicable to higher education.

The institution defines the time available for student learning experiences. Institutional allocations of time include such policies as:

- the length of the academic unit (semesters, quarters, or some other designation)
- the length and number of class periods per day and the length of time between classes
- the length and number of classes in the Core Curriculum, majors and minors
- the placement and length of breaks and vacations
- the number of study days before exams and the length of the actual exam period itself

These formal structures provide the framework for the instructional use of time by faculty. In addition, the university allocates a time frame for academic and non-academic support service units and learning experiences beyond the classroom through the designation of hours for the library, laboratories, instructional and skills centers, child care centers, study spaces, and guidelines for a required number of faculty office hours.

Each institution, driven by varying educational philosophies, political interests, and historical precedents allocates time differently. What is most important to consider in relation to the time on task principle, however, is that how time is allocated influences both how much and how well students learn. Institutions need to examine their own assumptions about time, and by extension, time on task. It is likely that these assumptions may be found to be based more upon administrative convenience and external appearance than on pedagogy. As Terenzini and Pascarella (1994) point out, "The bureaucratization of collegiate structures is a creature of administrative convenience and budgetary expedience. It surely has not evolved from any conception of how students learn, nor is it supported by research evidence" (p. 32).

One of the most pervasive myths surrounding time on university campuses is that while having students devote considerable time to the task of earning their degree is desirable, the time devoted to this task should not exceed four years. While this is possible for some students, for increasing numbers of students—especially older than average students—this assumption is inappropriate. To use the percentage of students who graduate in four years as a time on task indicator of a quality institution misapplies this principle and ignores the diversity of the college population.

### Instructor Use of Time

While the time available for instruction is defined by the university, how that time is used varies by instructor. Differences in manner and efficiency of presentation of materials, the frequency of unrelated tangents, and the time that the instructor begins and ends the class all influence the amount of time available for a student to be fully engaged in the learning process. More importantly though, the implementation of the other principles (cooperative learning, prompt feedback, student-faculty interaction, active learning, high expectations, and respect for diverse talents) influence the *quality* of the time spent learning. Instructors need to engage their students in the learning process, not allow them to simply "mark time" in the classroom.

Engaging students during the class period requires instructors to make the new information relevant to the learners, to use multiple methods of instruction, and to continually focus on helping their students understand. Faculty need to have a clear idea of the goals they hope to accomplish in each class period and use the class time available the best way they can to achieve that goal. To promote optimal use of time on task outside of the classroom, instructors should provide suggestions on the best way to study the material, identify resources which might be of assistance, be specific in terms of what should be accomplished by the next class meeting, and break down large projects into smaller tasks with intermediate deadlines which are perceived by students as being more manageable.

Finally, faculty need to demonstrate their own respect for the principle of time on task. If deadlines for student papers are strictly enforced, then faculty must be willing to dedicate the time on task necessary to ensure that feedback is prompt. Moreover, genuine concern for student learning needs to be demonstrated not only through prompt feedback, but also through faculty availability to students (e.g., regular office hours and availability for informal discussions).

## Student Use of Time

There is no magic number of hours that students should study in order to maximize learning. The *right* amount of time is the amount of time that it is necessary for students to achieve their personal learning goals and meet the goals of their assignments. If we are truly going to respect the diversity in our classrooms and at our universities, we need to understand that students require different amounts of time on any particular project or assignment.

Virtually all faculty members have heard students plead their case on a poorly performed test or assignment by arguing "I spent fifteen hours studying for the test " (or writing the paper). The rationale is specious. We all know that the amount of time isn't the issue. It's how that time was spent that makes the difference, and many students don't know how to use their time appropriately. Opportunities for students to improve their time management and study skills should be part of every student development program.

Time management and study skills are only part of the solution to improving our students' time on task. The efforts of colleges and universities to create a diverse population of traditional and non-traditional learners as well as the economic realities facing all students have created a population for whom achieving time on task is a significant challenge. Neither better teaching methods, higher expectations, or increased faculty interaction will be able to alleviate the strain many of our students face when trying to balance significant demands of families, jobs, and careers while pursuing their college educations. Although educators agree that time on task is a vital component to learning, many of today's students seem unable to devote sufficient time to their studies. Students need help balancing these demands, and universities can help by providing facilities and resources for students to make the most of the time that they have available.

## Summary

Time on task is a principle which is frequently taken for granted. As a result, it may not be receiving much institutional attention. More faculty, administrators, students, and other members of the higher education community need to understand as well as develop sound practices for maximizing quality time on task for the student. Thinking not only about how much time, but also how the time is spent, is a valuable approach to the assessment of the learning experience. It exhibits the potential of demonstrating the relationship between input and output—effort and achievement in student learning.

## Time On Task at Northeast Missouri State

What are some behaviors which seem to differentiate successful students with high time on task quotients from others? Northeast Missouri State University's study of the Political Science seniors suggests that these students (1) commit a comparatively high number of hours to study in and out of the classroom, (2) take notes from, or summarize, the reading assignments, (3) do not allow their peers to have a negative impact on their study time, (4) live on campus, and (5) avoid 'off task' behaviors in the classroom. Most students, successful or not, tend to take notes from lectures, do the reading (sooner or later), and review and/or practice before tests.

Northeast Missouri's Political Science study noted a strong negative correlation between grade point average and certain off-task behaviors (e.g., missing class and daydreaming once there). This suggests that the more successful students, in terms of GPA, are those who attend classes more regularly and are able to keep their attention focused on class activities more often. Obviously these observations are related to engaged time, and institutions and their instructors need to develop means to reinforce the related positive behaviors.

A problem with earlier studies was the failure to broaden the output or product variable beyond grade point average. At Northeast, other measures of student accomplishment have been the Major Field Assessment Test (MFAT) as well as a local test generated by the Political Science Faculty as part of a capstone experience. The initial discovery within the data is that students with high GPAs tend to do well on both of these tests. This finding can be interpreted to mean that those students who go to the effort of building a strong GPA class by class tend to demonstrate greater learning (as measured by these tests) than do those who show lesser commitment. Why is this important? Many students' career paths depend on evidence of undergraduate success. These students need to be made aware that their performance in each class has an impact on the most commonly used indicators. In other words, their future may be at stake.

Test scores were affected positively by the number of hours students had taken in political science. Faculty members and administrators may be interested in attempting to identify a critical threshold (if there is one)—i.e., the number of major courses needed to ensure a good chance of success on the exams. In addition, students who demonstrated better study habits (e.g., reading on schedule, taking notes on reading and lectures regularly, reviewing for exams and missing few if any classes) tended to do better on the exams. Once again, the steady performance seems to pay off. Those students "guilty" of significant levels of off-task behavior tended to score lower on the tests.

The NMSU study also indicates that students who productively apply the time on task principles at Northeast tend to practice the accompanying behaviors as early as high school or even junior high school. It apparently takes a while to effectively incorporate these time on task patterns into student lifestyles.

The NMSU study shows a strong correlation between students who take a broad time on task swath of university life and students who are satisfied with the institution and its environment. Participation in frequent experiences relative to the library, faculty interaction, cultural refinement, athletics or recreation, the student union, clubs, and even conversations tended to deepen the value of the institution to the students as well as improve academic performance in a variety of ways.

## Time on Task: The Principle in Action

Where does one look in order to see the time on task in action? There are a number of institutions around the nation which demonstrate a high level of time on task consciousness. This consciousness is evidenced through innovative scheduling, study in depth, and assistance in time management skills.

## *Time for Learning*

Many colleges and universities have worked to create more time for learning. In the most dramatic instance, this required a significant restructuring of the curriculum.

- Evergreen State College has developed of a series of year-long coordinated studies programs. The basic assumption of this approach is that traditional discrete courses have become a primary hindrance to meaningful undergraduate education. To counteract the perceived problems, faculty and administrators at Evergreen involved themselves in a "radical restructuring" of the curriculum which attacked the traditional class schedule and opened up various possibilities for extended learning experiences utilizing longer blocks of time. These incorporate team teaching and interdisciplinary themes. Typically, three faculty members provide about 60 students with a program characterized as highly sequenced and specific with respect to content and skills development. Learning activities for this program include a variety of large and small group strategies. For their part, students receive sixteen credits per quarter. In addition, they receive credit in English composition, physical anthropology, the history of science, and economics.

  Barbara Leigh Smith, Provost & Academic Vice President
  Evergreen State College
  Olympia, WA 95805
  (206) 866-6400
  FAX (206) 866-6823

- "Innovative Month" programs at Fort Lewis College in Colorado expand allocated time. Students are offered a series of five-week summer domestic and foreign travel experiences designed to help them explore applications of classroom learning in real life settings. The travel groups are limited in number from eight to fifteen students per faculty member. Examples of Innovative Programs include, "Management in Action," "Native American Schools," and "Music and Theatre in England."

Betty Perry
Vice President of Academic Affairs
Fort Lewis College
Durango, CO 81301
(303) 247-7010

- Mississippi State offers an intensive, three-week "Sea-Earth-Sky" program at the end of the spring semester. This course, designed by the biology and art departments, emphasizes the links between the biological, ecological, environmental, and economic aspects of the Gulf Coast and inculcates an appreciation of the natural world. The biology and art components are offered in tandem, seven days a week, beginning at 7 a.m. and lasting into mid-evening, with breaks for lunch and dinner. Both combine traditional classroom learning on campus with on-site study at and around Mississippi's Gulf Coast Research Laboratory, less than a five-hour drive from campus.

Douglas Feig, Associate Dean, College of Arts and Sciences
Mississippi State University, Drawer AS
Mississippi State, MS 39762
(601) 325-2645

### Study in Depth

Even within a traditional course schedule, it is possible to maximize the time available for learning through coordinated clusters of classes or sequences of courses over several terms.

- At Lower Columbia College, the Integrative Studies Program is a block of 15 to 18 credit hours, organized around a theme. Students enroll in "traditional" courses, but must enroll in the full block. The faculty team is free to reorganize the day from the traditional fifty-minute meeting schedule to include whatever schedule of lectures, seminars, conferences, and discussion groups is needed to achieve learning objectives for that week.

Donald E. Fuller, Ph.D., Dean of Instruction
Lower Columbia College
P.O. Box 3010
Longview, WA 98632
(206) 577-3428

- LaGuardia Community College (CUNY) requires liberal arts majors to participate in an introductory liberal arts cluster. The typical cluster consists of a three-credit freshman composition course, a two-credit course in writing research papers, and two additional humanities and/or social science courses that provide the "content" of the cluster. Clusters are loosely based upon one of two themes—individual freedom and the role of work in our lives.

  Harriet Mesulam and Roberta Matthews
  Office of Academic Affairs
  LaGuardia Community College
  31-10 Thomson Avenue
  Long Island City, NY 11101
  (718) 482-5414; (718) 482-5405

- Bard College's Freshman Workshop in Language and Thinking helps students become more fluent and effective writers and more engaged and self-directed learners. The Freshman Workshop is conducted in three ninety-minute sessions per day, five and one-half days per week, for three weeks in August. With a faculty recruited nationally for its experience in writing instruction, the Workshop emphasizes collaborative learning among students.

  Paul Connolly, Director, and Teresa Vilardi, Director
  The Institute for Writing and Thinking
  102 Ludlow, Bard College
  Annandale-on-Hudson, NY 12504
  (914) 758-7432

- Skagit Valley College requires all students to take two learning-community programs as part of the Associate of Arts degree. These range from linked classes combining skill courses with content courses to full-time coordinated studies programs.

  Brinton Sprague, Vice President
  Skagit Valley College
  2405 College Way
  Mount Vernon, WA 98273
  (206) 428-1223

• Honors students at Western Michigan University typically take two clusters, the first during the fall of the freshman year, the second during their sophomore year. The courses linked through the cluster carry general education or major credit and usually meet requirements in specific college curricula.

> Joseph G. Reish, Dean
> The Lee Honors College
> Western Michigan University
> Kalamazoo, MI 49008
> (616) 387-3230

• Linked courses at North Seattle Community College consist of two or more courses scheduled back-to-back, with the content of one reinforcing and utilizing the other. The program is scheduled in large blocks of time, rather than 50 minute periods.

> Dr. Thomas Griffith, Associate Dean
> Science, Math and College Curriculum
> North Seattle Community College
> 900 College Way North
> Seattle, WA 98103
> (206) 527-3747

• Recognizing low enrollment of women and certain minority students in freshman calculus (a gateway course for the rest of the sciences), the Seattle Central Community College faculty integrate material from the normal four-quarter sequence into a two-quarter course. Students with this "double dose" of calculus are able to focus more intensively on the subject, moving into calculus rapidly. The intensity of this effort is reinforced by students working in groups both inside and outside of class.

> Janet P. Ray, Mathematics Department
> Seattle Central Community College
> 1701 Broadway
> Seattle, WA 98122
> (206) 587-4080
> e-mail: jray@guest.nwnet.net

## Encouraging Students to Use Time Effectively

Institutions have assisted students in meeting their time on task challenges by encouraging the development of time management skills.

- Mississippi University for Women uses its University 101 course to put into place a tracking system in core-curriculum courses to monitor student progress and intervene as necessary to keep students "on task." The course itself includes significant focus on study habits, the value of time on task, and effective time management techniques to try to help students make the adjustments to the demands of college-level work. Instructors are encouraged to contact students who miss class excessively and to report the problem to the students' advisers. Mid-term grades are sent to allow time for academic counseling or other assistance as necessary. Finally, time-on-task counseling is available to students at all levels.

  M.L. Petty
  Mississippi University for Women
  W/Box 1624
  Columbus, MS 39701
  (601) 329-7129

- At Wake Forest University, time management and study skills are taught by the Learning Assistance Program as well as in the Learning to Learn course on campus. Through a counseling/teaching model in the Learning Assistance Program, students are individually encouraged to learn and develop strategies to improve their academic performance. In the Learning to Learn course, first and second year students study learning theory with emphasis on demonstrating how good time management and appropriate study skills positively affect outcome.

  Dr. Sandra Chadwick, Director
  Learning Assistance Program
  Wake Forest University
  P.O. Box 7283
  Reynolds Station
  Winston-Salem, NC 27109
  e-mail: chadwick@ac.wfunet.sfu.edu

*Stuart Vorkink is Professor of Political Science, Northeast Missouri State University.*

## References

Geiger, K. (1994). Rethinking school time: New, better, and different...as well as more. *The Washington Post,* June 12, 1994. p. C3.

Terenzini, P. T., and Pascarella, E.T. (1994). Living with myths: Undergraduate education in America". *Change* , pp. 28–32.

## Resources: Time on Task

Britton, B. K., and Tesser, A. (1991). Effects of time management practices on college grades. *Journal of Educational Psychology,* 83 (3), 405–410.

Earth-sea-sky course combines art, science: Mississippi State University. (1988). *Liberal Education,* 74 (2), 29–30.

Ludewig, L. M. (1992). The ten commandments for effective study skills. *The Teaching Professor,* 6 (10), 3.

**Principle 6: Good Practice Communicates High Expectations**

*Expect more and you will get it. High expectations are important for everyone—for the poorly prepared, for those unwilling to exert themselves, and for the bright and motivated. Expecting students to perform well becomes a self-fulfilling prophecy when teachers and institutions hold high expectations of themselves and make extra efforts.*

6

# EFFECTIVE UNDERGRADUATE EDUCATION COMMUNICATES HIGH EXPECTATIONS

*Robert A. Scott and Dorothy Echols Tobe*

## High Expectations: An Overview

Frank Newman, president of the Education Commission of the States, told the graduating students of Worcester Polytechnic Institute:

> *"The Commission spent the last year…gathering every bit of research we could find on whether all students can, in fact, learn. It turns out they all can. What inhibits them are the expectations we have for them. We now assume that every student has a finite ability, and that the primary job of the education system is sorting, not educating. But our future depends on education, not sorting." (An American Agenda: Transforming Primary and Secondary Education in United States, Worcester Polytechnic Institute Commencement, May 18, 1991).*

Though often talked about only at the instructional level, the high expectations principle concerns students' performance and behavior both inside and outside of the classroom. Colleges and universities want students to meet the high expectations set for performance in their classes. But high expectations also include a personal and professional commitment to sound values and ethics. They include the discipline to set goals and stick with them, an awareness and appreciation of the diversity of society, and a philosophy of service to others.

### All Students Can Achieve

We know from studies in social psychology that high achieving students are those who identify themselves as "school learners." Success in school is part of their self-definition. These students are able and willing to measure themselves against school values and goals, in part because they feel that they are treated as a valued person with good chances of success. Individuals determine who they are from the way they are treated by "significant others" in their lives. If an individual is to have a strong sense of self as a "learner" or student, he or she needs respect and encouragement from those important others.

Not all students enter college with this level of confidence in themselves as learners. Many—especially African-Americans, lower-class Caucasians, Hispanics, and women in male-dominated fields—often feel stigmatized as students and need encouragement. Many have come through the elementary and secondary systems without a positive sense of who they are or what they can achieve. The work of Philip Uri Treisman at Berkeley, Jaime Escalante in East Los Angeles, and James Comer at Yale, among others, supports the notion that learning and raised expectations require a strong "accepting" relationship between student and teacher. As Claude Steele (1992) points out in *Atlantic Monthly*, the student must feel that teachers or professors expect high performance because they believe the student is capable of it and that they will reward the student for success.

A campus-wide approach to effective undergraduate education communicates high expectations and encourages high aspirations in students by making high expectations a college-wide goal, and by challenging students to set goals, aim high, and achieve. This approach to education challenges students appropriately, offers encouragement, and provides reinforcement from faculty, staff, college activities, and policies. It also encourages students to become active as learners and participants.

This approach to student development contrasts starkly with the old "look on your right, look on your left" orientation at large universities and practiced at most institutions not long ago. The old approach expressed negative expectations: "Two-thirds of you won't make it; the odds are against you!" The new approach expresses positive expectations, and provides follow-through as well.

## Individualizing Expectations

High expectations alone will not automatically result in higher student aspirations and higher student achievement. Talent, motivation, and experience must be present in students in order for "high expectations" to produce results. But many times, native talent is left to languish because interest is not encouraged and experiences are denied.

And, of course, not all students have equal talent. So any amount of teacher encouragement for high achievement will be moderated by the student's talent and ability, as affected by both nature and nurture. However, all students can do better, even if not equally well, and the role of the teacher is to encourage improvement, not expect equal results of all.

Several steps can be taken to help all students achieve. While the most important step is the creation of a classroom climate that encourages success, essential steps include the articulation of clear expectations of student performance, allowing assignments to be tailored to meet specific needs and interests, modeling excellent work, providing feedback on works in progress, accepting mistakes, and celebrating successes. All of these steps contribute to the achievement of high expectations by all students, while at the same time encouraging cooperation, fostering motivation, and respecting the diverse talents of the class members.

## Helping All Students Succeed

*Supportive Climate.* A supportive classroom climate is critical to student achievement. It fosters achievement because students are more willing to stretch themselves in new directions, without fear of failure or embarrassment. A supportive classroom environment gives permission to students to be bold, daring, and creative in their assignments because there is respect for the learning process and a high level of trust between and among students and faculty members.

There are two significant threats to creating a supportive climate. First, there is the perception of competition. As Chapter 2 pointed out, when students feel that they are competing with each other for a limited number of rewards—usually good grades—both cooperation and motivation suffer. If a faculty member really believes in the ability of *each* student to succeed, then there can be no limit to the number of rewards. Each student in the class can "win." All students are motivated to excel, because each knows there is potential reward.

The second threat to creating a supportive climate is the perception among students that they are being "ambushed" by an assignment. Students know the instructor holds high expectations for their performance, but the exact expectations and the evaluation criteria are sometimes unclear. Students in this situation genuinely don't know when they turn in an assignment whether or not it meets the instructor's expectations. And they don't find out until after the assignment has been given a final grade, without opportunity to rewrite or rework once the criteria have become clear.

*Clear Expectations of Performance.* Students need to know what is expected of them. It is up to both the institution and individual faculty members to make clear their expectations of students' performance and behavior. These expectations should be part of every recruiting brochure. First-year student orientation, as well as co-curricular and extra-curricular programs and activities should reinforce these high expectations.

Course policies and expectations of out-of-class commitment to the class need to be articulated early in each course. A logical place is in the course syllabus. In addition, each assignment needs to be described in such a way that students understand the expected standard of performance and the criteria against which their work will be evaluated. One idea is to distribute grading criteria with each assignment. The criteria description outlines the characteristics of "outstanding," "good," "acceptable," and "unacceptable" work on that assignment.

*Tailoring Assignments to Meet Individual Needs and Interests.* Not all students enter each class with a similar set of talents, interests, and achievements. Because students are so different, allowing students flexibility to tailor classes to their particular needs and interests is essential. These options allow students opportunities to highlight their individual interests, talents, and accomplishments. In an interviewing class, for example, students may create their own hypothetical interviewing scenarios for role play, allowing the assignment to be tailored to each student's personal needs and professional goals. A journalism student, for example, may create a series of information-gathering interviews for role play, while a management major might create scenarios dealing with hiring and performance appraisals.

*Modeling.* Telling students what constitutes excellent work is helpful; showing them is powerful. Providing models of outstanding student papers and videotapes of exemplary student speeches or presentations provides the student with a clear idea of how the expectations translate into a finished product. The evidence that other students—students just like them—have done excellent work is a strong motivator. In addition, faculty members and institutions need to hold themselves accountable to the high expectations of their students. Modeling works both ways.

*Feedback on Works in Progress.* Prompt feedback (Chapter 4) is an essential part of achieving high expectations. Students need to have the opportunity to receive feedback along the way. In fact, receiving 'intermediate' feedback should be a required part of a course. Quizzes, application papers, exercises, activities, or submissions of drafts of major papers can all be designed to let students know if they are on the right track.

*Tolerate Mistakes.* Everyone can be counted on to make a mistake now and then. High expectations do not require that all students be perfect. A supportive environment encourages students to keep pushing, to do better, to succeed, even if early attempts are unsuccessful. Multiple opportunities for success must exist.

*Celebrate Success.* As Boyer points out in his book, *Campus Life: In Search of Community*, one of the characteristics of a community is that it is "celebrative." Student achievements should be celebrated both within a sponsoring department and throughout the campus. The celebration becomes yet another motivator to students, showing again that high expectations can be achieved.

## Summary

Students must experience raised expectations, whether through internal motivation or external encouragement, to be successful learners. However, raised expectations are not limited to the classroom. According to George Kuh of Indiana University, "healthy campus communities expect participation and sharing of leadership tasks." Goals for high expectations should be enumerated for students as individuals as well as for students as members of the campus community seeking a sense of "wholeness." Such goals should be defined so that they can be monitored and measured by both quantitative and qualitative methods. Goals can be communicated by campus practices which require attendance policies, encourage study skills sessions and tutors for students who need them, and uphold prerequisite requirements. We must develop an "air of expectancy," that can be reflected in student achievement and involvement.

## Applications at Ramapo College of New Jersey

At Ramapo College, many of our students are the first in their families to attend college, and many have a rather limited educational vision. They want something practical that will lead to a job; we want to help them prepare for a series of stages in several careers. In addition to these low expectations, students often come with relatively low self-esteem as academic achievers and the classic profile of "late bloomers." For these reasons, the college actually substitutes for the family and community by expressing heightened expectations for academic and professional accomplishment. Therefore, an education that "transforms" the individual is particularly important. While the activities related to raising aspirations are decentralized throughout the campus, in each one we seek to "engage" students in a proactive manner.

Mentoring is a concept that personalizes education and is a program that is particularly well-suited for a small campus. Since we know that all students can learn, the one-to-one relationships that develop from faculty mentoring can have a strong impact on student development

Our mentoring activities are as diverse as our student body. The Minority Achievement Program seeks to bridge academic learning with career choices beyond college. Mentors from the corporate community and our Ramapo College Foundation Board of Governors are selected to work with students in the "spirit of inquisitiveness"—what do you do, how is it done, where, etc. This program is geared to students of color, and through these interactions they learn to trust those who are different from themselves and to earn affirmation from these mentors as well as from those who are similar. Since the program's inception in 1984, we can count a number of success stories, including a high retention and graduation rate for the student participants.

Faculty involvement is key to any higher aspirations program, for it is through them that students build their self-esteem and raise their aspirations. It is through faculty that college expectations are communicated and encouraged. They help to build the "campus climate" with respect to higher aspiration goals. Members of the faculty have agreed to mentor students—both those who are self-selected, and therefore motivated, and those who are in serious academic difficulty.

An example of faculty mentoring at work includes a student who had been dismissed from the college. He appealed the decision to the Office of the Vice President for Academic Affairs. This student's academic record was abysmal, but during his appeal, he communicated a sincere willingness to take an active interest in his education. The college took him at his word and decided to re-admit him with the provision that he find a faculty member who would work with him one-to-one throughout the semester. He found someone willing to mentor him and achieved a 4.0 grade point average taking twelve credits. He had the preparation and ability; he needed motivation and encouragement.

## High Expectations: The Principle in Action

Examples of activities to raise student expectations for their own achievement may be found at all types of institutions throughout the country.

### Setting and Communicating Expectations

Vital to the achievement of high expectations is the setting and communicating of these expectations to students, faculty and staff.

- The University of North Carolina-Asheville advises prospective faculty during the hiring process that their major responsibility will be to teach undergraduate students consistent with the campus mission; that departments are seeking faculty who will be "institutional colleagues" willing to teach general education courses and not simply become enmeshed in their private scholarship. Faculty also are advised to encourage students to participate in research projects and, when possible, to urge students to present research results at conferences with the faculty member.

> Larry Wilson
> Vice Chancellor of Academic Affairs
> University of North Carolina-Asheville
> One University Heights
> Asheville, NC 28804-3299
> (704) 251-6600

- New faculty in the Great Lakes Colleges Association (GLCA) —a consortium of twelve private liberal arts and sciences institutions in Indiana, Michigan and Ohio—are paired with senior faculty mentors at GLCA institutions other than their own, in an effort to promote professional development. This program helps faculty new to teaching by assisting them in the transition from a graduate school environment to one with high expectations for classroom teaching and student advising.

> Michelle D. Gilliard, GLCA Program Associate
> 2929 Plymouth Road, Suite 207
> Ann Arbor, MI 48105
> (313) 761-4833

- Students at Grinnell College become acquainted with Grinnell's educational philosophy through the college catalogue, student handbook, advising handbook, and faculty advisement. Each outlines the kinds of abilities and knowledge believed to constitute a liberally educated person. In addition, students learn Grinnell's academic expectations in the summer preceding their first semester. All entering students select a Freshman Research and Writing Tutorial. The tutorial contributes significantly to Grinnell's advising system.

Charles Duke, VP Academic Affairs and Dean of Faculty
Grinnell College
P. O. Box 805
Grinnell, IA 50112
(515) 269-3100

- Students in the Introductory Psychology course at Bellevue University (Nebraska) are introduced on their syllabi to a list of suggestions for answering essay questions. These suggestions are designed to provide direction in responding to a broadly stated essay problem. Students are then given three exams during the course. The first two exams include the list of suggestions as well as the essay question; the third exam includes only the essay question. Students are allowed the opportunity to "practice" their writing skills until prompting is no longer necessary.

Cyril J. Leise
Bellevue University
1000 Galvin Road South
Bellevue, NE 68005
(402) 293-3737
e-mail: cjl@ns.ccsn.edu

- At Pepperdine University in California, students in communication classes know exactly what is expected of them. On the first day of class, the instructor distributes a set of grade profiles which describes what the professor feels are characteristics of outstanding, above average, and typical students. The grade profiles identify the student's attendance, preparation, curiosity, retention, attitudes, talent, and results as key variables impacting the student's final grade.

John H. Williams
Pepperdine University
Malibu, CA 90265
(310) 456-4000

- Students who are taking courses in French Language or French Literature at Davidson College know that their instructor expects 100% attendance. Students who are chronically late or absent might expect a visit from the entire class who will serenade the student with "Frère Jacques."

Everett F. Jacobus Jr.
Davidson College
Davidson, NC 28036

Faculty aren't the only ones who have expectations. Students also enter college or universities with expectations.

- First-year student expectations were collected during new student orientation at Lakehead University in Thunder Bay. Students reported expectations which included large amounts of homework, unapproachable professors, financial problems, low grades, large and boring classes, and difficulty in making friends. Understanding students' initial negative expectations can help faculty deal with them before they become self-fulfilling prophecies.

Jane Crossman, Physical Education
Ken Brown, Forestry
Lakehead University
Thunder Bay, ON P7B 5E1
(807) 343-8110

## High Expectations and General Education

General education programs are one way colleges and universities articulate their expectations of the essential skills, abilities, knowledge, and values which all of their students should be able to demonstrate. Some notable programs and requirements are listed below.

- Grinnell College doesn't require a particular general education sequence or any distribution requirements. Instead, their philosophy is to make clear the college's expectations and back up their expectations with a strong advising system. Grinnell's catalogue suggests components of a model curriculum and includes course combinations to meet individuals' interests and career aspirations.

Charles Duke, VP Academic Affairs and Dean of Faculty
Grinnell College
P. O. Box 805
Grinnell, IA 50112
(515) 269-3100

- The Community Life program at Mars Hill College requires students to attend forty cultural and intellectual events in four years.

  Dr. Larry Stern, Director of Institutional Research
  Mars Hill College
  Mars Hill, NC 28754
  (704) 689-1439

- University requirements at Sonoma State University call for all students to complete 48 units in the areas of communication and critical thinking, natural science and mathematics, arts and humanities, and social sciences. While most students fulfill their general education requirements through traditional disciplinary subjects, four courses in the Hutchins School of Liberal Studies, using an interdisciplinary, seminar-based approach, satisfy all but one of the lower-division requirements.

  Les Adler, Provost
  Hutchins School of Liberal Studies
  Sonoma State University
  Rohnert Park, CA 94928
  (707) 664-2491
  Fax (707) 664-2505

## Reinforcing Expectations

Though colleges and universities can promote high expectations for student performance, responsibility for internalizing these expectations ultimately rests on individual students.

- At the University of Maine at Farmington, faculty are engaged in a long-term project to address issues of American pluralism not as "multiculturalism," but in terms of the conflict of values facing students who come from homes and environments where intellectual aspirations are not encouraged. This allows students to explore and embrace the liberalizing effects of education and to identify and articulate those values they have subscribed to prior to enrollment. Students can contrast them with those which other students bring to college, leading to new perspectives and elevated aspirations.

Frank Doran
Vice President of Academic Affairs
University of Maine at Farmington
Farmington, ME 04938
(207) 778-7000

Other examples include the University of Oregon's freshman interest groups, Eastern Washington University's freshman studies, Western Michigan University's cluster groupings, LaGuardia Community College's learning clusters, and SUNY-Stony Brook's federated learning communities. The goals of these efforts are to raise student performance in terms of retention, grade point average, intellectual achievements, and graduation.

## Monitoring Progress and Measuring Goals

It is up to each institution to define what constitutes achievement of the expectations identified for students. While at many colleges achievement of expectations is evidenced simply by a student receiving a passing grade in identified courses, other institutions go further by assessing a student's level of mastery against a set of specific expectations.

- In the liberal arts core sequence at Alverno College, faculty have defined sequential levels of mastery that all undergraduates must develop and demonstrate in the context of varied disciplines. At each successive level, the expectations for student performance increase until, at level four, students can demonstrate increasing integration of the abilities and knowledge that contribute to general education. Students generally achieve the four levels within the first two years of college. They then demonstrate an additional two levels in the context of their major fields, with level six requiring independent ability to apply all the accumulated skills and knowledge in professional situations.

Kathleen O'Brien, Academic Dean
Alverno College, 3401 South 39th St.
P.O. Box 343922
Milwaukee, WI 53234-3922
(414) 382-6084

- At Clayton State College, students are expected to exhibit seven different writing abilities. There are several levels of proficiency for each of the seven criteria. All students must pass writing assessments on four different occasions in their careers at Clayton State.

  Dr. Brad Rice, Assistant VP Academic Affairs
  Clayton State College
  Morrow, GA 30260
  (404) 961-3581

- In order to understand how students at SUNY-Plattsburgh learn and develop and how the school can help them to do so, students are required to take the College Outcomes Measures Project examination of the American College Testing Program (ACT COMP) as freshmen and again at the end of the sophomore year.

  E. Thomas Moran, Vice President of Academic Affairs
  SUNY-Plattsburgh
  Plattsburgh, NY 12901
  (518) 564-2080

- At the University of Colorado at Denver, students can chart their learning progress through the use of a Monster Exam. A faculty member in geology compiles all of the exam questions from the last time he taught the course. This 'monster exam' is given to students the first day of class. Students are asked to indicate which questions they already know the answers to, which questions they know where to find the answer, and which questions they do not know where to begin looking for the answer. As course material is covered, the instructor refers back to the monster exam, and at the end of the course, students take it again, coding answers as they did the first day of class. Before and after surveys show students exactly what they have learned during the course.

  Edward B. Nuhfer
  University of Colorado at Denver
  1250 14th St.
  P.O. Box 73364
  Denver, CO 80217-3364
  (303) 556-2400

## Incentives and Rewards for Raised Expectations

Many opportunities exist to recognize students and faculty who have fulfilled higher aspirations, and those faculty and staff who have supported them.

- Ramapo College acknowledges noteworthy students, faculty, and staff achievements at orientation, at each semester's all-college convocation, at Honors Convocations, at Deans' Award Dinners, at Trustee meetings, at graduation, and at other times and in various publications. By using highly visible occasions to discuss the importance of high aspirations, the college conveys both higher expectations and a willingness to reward those who try.

  Ron Kase
  Assoc. Vice President of Academic Affairs
  Ramapo College of New Jersey
  505 Ramapo Valley Rd.
  Mahwah, NJ 07430
  (201) 529-7731

- Each year, the Disabled Students' Organization at Ball State University honors faculty members who have provided innovative, flexible, and adaptive classroom instructions for students with disabilities. "The Most Accessible Teacher" award is not given to the teacher whom disabled students find the "easiest," but instead is given to those faculty members whom students find to have been the most demanding, who have challenged them and held them accountable while providing flexible, innovative, and reasonable accommodations.

  Richard Harris
  Director of the Office of Disabled Student Development
  Ball State University
  Muncie, IN 47306
  (317) 285-5293

## Summary

The mission of higher education is to enhance the ability of students to learn now, and to become lifelong learners. We do that by providing an environment that offers encouragement, provides reinforcement, and challenges students to set goals, aim high, and achieve. In order for students to fulfill these goals, they must be highly motivated and have the skills necessary to advance. In other words, a campus-wide approach to effective undergraduate education communicates high expectations, and in turn, encourages high aspirations and achievement from students.

*Robert A. Scott is President, Ramapo College of New Jersey, and a founding president of the Council of Public Liberal Arts Colleges.*

*Dorothy Echols Tobe is Associate Vice President for Administration and Finance, and has taught as an adjunct professor in Social Sciences and Human Services, Ramapo College of New Jersey.*

## References

"An American agenda: Transforming primary and secondary education in United States." Worcester Polytechnic Institute Commencement, May 18, 1991, p. 4.

Boyer. E. (1990). *Campus Life: In Search of Community. A Special Report.* Lawrenceville, NJ: Princeton University Press.

Kuh, G. D. (1991). The role of admissions and orientation in creating appropriate expectations for college life. *College and University,* 66 (2), 75–82.

Steele, C. M. (1992). Race and schooling of black Americans. *The Atlantic Monthly,* pp. 68–78.

## Resources: High Expectations

*An American Imperative: Higher Expectations for Higher Education.* An open letter to those concerned about the American future. Report of the Wingspread group in Higher education. (1993).

Crossman, J., and Brown, K. (1993). First year fears. *The Teaching Professor,* 7 (2), 5.

Defining what students need to know: Clayton State. (1988). *Liberal Education,* 74 (3), 29–30.

Emphasizing what students can do with what they know: Alverno College. (1988). *Liberal Education,* 74 (3), 27–29.

Exit interviews for graduates: Drew University. (1987). *Liberal Education ,* 73 (3), 29–31.

Freedom of choice encourages active learning: Grinnell College. (1988). *Liberal Education,* 74 (4), 27–28.

Gabelnick, F., MacGregor, J., Matthews, R.S., and Smith, B. L. (1990). Learning communities: Creative connections among students, faculty and disciplines. *New Directions for Teaching and Learning,* (4), San Francisco, CA: Jossey-Bass.

Helping disabled students help themselves: Ball State University. (1990). *Liberal Education,* 76 (3), 30–31.

Humanities bring coherence to general education curriculum: Mars Hill College. (1988). *Liberal Education,* 74 (5), 31–33.

Jacobus, E. F. Jr. (1993). All present and accounted for. *The Teaching Professor,* 7 (3), 4.

Kuh, G. D. (1991). Snapshots of a campus community. *Educational Record,* p. 43.

Nuhfer, E. B. (1993). Bottom line disclosure and assessment. *The Teaching Professor,* 7 (7), 8.

Program fosters faculty mentoring: Great Lakes Colleges Association. (1990). *Liberal Education,* 76 (3), 34–36.

Scott, R. A. (1993). Student learning: The priority for the future. *Higher Education & National Affairs,* ACE.

Scott, R. A. (1993). The president as philosopher. *Liberal Education,* 79 (3), 51–53.

Value added project in early stages: SUNY Plattsburgh. (1987). *Liberal Education,* 73 (3), 2931–33.

Williams, J. H. (1993). Clarifying grade expectations. *The Teaching Professor,* 7 (7), 1.

**Principle 7: Good Practice Respects Diverse Talents and Ways of Learning**

*There are many roads to learning. People bring different talents and styles of learning to college. Brilliant students in the seminar room may be all thumbs in the lab or art studio. Students rich in hands-on experience may not do so well with theory. Students need the opportunity to show their talents and learn in ways that work for them. Then they can be pushed to learning in ways that do not come so easily.*

7

# GOOD PRACTICE RESPECTS DIVERSE TALENTS AND WAYS OF LEARNING

*Russell M. Lidman, Barbara Leigh Smith, and Thomas L. Purce*

## Respecting Diversity: An Overview

Effective institutions are clear about what diversity means. They embrace diversity and systematically cultivate it. They see diversity as a critical feature of their environment. They understand and respect each student as an individual with a unique set of talents and abilities and work hard to accommodate the differences among learners. This doesn't suggest that each college can be all things to all people nor that all forms of diversity can be accommodated. There is, however, an appropriate balance. The challenge for universities is to remain sensitive to and accommodate as many of the diverse needs of its students and faculty as possible. Respect for diversity should play a central part in university decisions, be apparent in the services and resources available to students, be a feature of every academic program, and practiced in every classroom.

## Diversity Matters

Diversity matters because academe is changing. Our educational institutions need to reflect and to prepare students for this changing world. Several factors make diversity important today:

- The increasing demographic diversity in our population and in the student population

- The increasingly international and interdependent character of our world

- The increasing recognition of the diverse ways in which people learn

We are living in a time of rapid change, a time in which the information base of our society and our educational institutions becomes quickly outmoded. It has been widely reported that this is a transitional period, moving from an industrial to an information society. Worldwide communications systems allow almost immediate access to events and ideas from around the globe. Rapid changes in technology and the information base of our society require new skills and ways of thinking.

As a result, there is less need for educational approaches that place emphasis on rote learning. Instead, education should place a premium on teaching the skills of learning—on learning how to learn. With this must come the recognition that people learn differently and no one method of teaching will touch all learners.

## Accommodating Demographic Diversity

The student body in America's schools is increasingly diverse in terms of age, gender, race, cultural and socioeconomic background, previous experience, and levels of preparation. Demographic diversity in terms of race is already a reality in many urban public schools: All ten of the largest urban school systems are now "majority minority" (Hodgkinson, 1985). This diversity will increase in the future. Designing instructional programs to accommodate diversity is a critical task, and effective colleges are occupied with it.

Increasing evidence proves that long-standing, conventional instructional methods are not succeeding as well as they should. Major efforts are underway to reform many of the traditional academic disciplines, from mathematics and the sciences to foreign language study as well as the social sciences and the humanities. It is increasingly clear that people learn in many different ways and current instructional modes teach to a narrow range of learning styles. Teaching and learning approaches that more actively engage the learner are seen by many as critical to reach the students of both today and tomorrow (see Bonnwell & Eison, 1991; Claxton & Murrell 1987). The effective school recognizes that students learn differently and acknowledges that fact in what is taught and how it is taught.

## *Dimensions of Diversity*

There are a number of key dimensions to examine in thinking about whether an institution nourishes diversity. It is possible to assess this through an examination of what the school means by "diversity," and how this commitment plays out in the culture, the academic processes and structures, and the spending decisions of an institution.

*Institutional Goals.* The effective institution recognizes and actively nurtures diverse talents and ways of learning. Diversity is a stated goal with clear definition, and it is played out in specific, tangible practices throughout the university.

*Organizational Culture.* The effective institution is flexible, willing to support the needs of the diverse population that it has created. In every school that has acknowledged the need for changes to accommodate their more diverse student population, there has been some discomfort and wrangling about the pace, direction, and economic consequences of that change. But if diversity really matters, these changes will be welcome as vital enhancements to the institution.

*Characteristics of the Faculty and Students.* The effective institution purposefully seeks out a diverse student body, faculty, and staff. This diversity is a resource for the curriculum, instruction, and student life in general.

*Characteristics of the Academic Programs.* Good practice recognizes that academic programs can both nurture and respond to diversity. Academic programs that contain a variety of experiences allowing for students to display their knowledge in a variety of ways demonstrate this principle.

*The Learning Process and Modes of Teaching and Learning.* Good practice recognizes that students learn in a variety of ways and values the process—as well as the outcomes—of learning. In the effective institution, pedagogy is varied. Besides conventional lecture classes, workshops, seminars, field experience, and/or independent study, among other modes, contribute to the learning process. The academic program should demonstrate its awareness and sensitivity to the diverse needs and talents of the population it serves, not be abstractly tolerant of them.

*Support for Risk-Taking.* Not all students start with the same attitude toward knowledge and learning. The effective institution will attempt to overcome the student's fear of approaching a body of knowledge as a novice, or the anxiety about acquiring new or higher-level competence. An institution that values diversity does not punish those who take academic risks. Alternative grading options and other procedures encourage academic risk-taking.

These factors overlap among themselves and with the other six principles. They speak to the challenges regarding diversity in our colleges and universities. It is increasingly clear that we need— and good practice requires— environments in which both the student and the institution learn.

## A College Designed Around Diversity: The Evergreen State College

The Evergreen State College is a public college of 3200 students located in Olympia, Washington. The college is officially recognized as the state's public liberal arts college, distinctively organized around an interdisciplinary curriculum and collaborative approaches to teaching and learning. Established in the late 1960's, Evergreen is one of the only so-called "alternative colleges" of that period that survived and flourished with its founding values and practices largely intact. Because the entire college was designed as an alternative institution, Evergreen had the singular opportunity to develop practices, organizational structures, and an academic culture that support this distinctive mission.

Evergreen embraces diversity in a variety of ways. It strives to be a diverse community in terms of its student body, faculty, and staff. And it has institutional practices that recognize that there are a variety of ways of learning and demonstrating one's academic growth. The college is student-centered. It places considerable responsibility upon students, and it organizes its instructional program around methods that require student involvement.

Like many colleges, Evergreen struggles to create a diverse student body. Rather than selecting students primarily on the basis of traditional measures such as grade point average or SAT scores, the college seeks a balanced student body from a national pool. Cultural diversity tuition waivers and academic programs on the Quinault Indian Reservation and in the African-American community of Tacoma enhance the college's capability to serve students of color.

Evergreen recognizes that a diverse faculty is also important. Nearly 40% of its faculty are women. One in four are people of color. The emphasis in faculty recruiting is to attract committed teachers with interdisciplinary skills and interests. The reward system reinforces a central commitment to teaching and collaborative inquiry.

In terms of pedagogical practice and academic program, Evergreen's structure is unusual. Instead of taking four traditional courses each quarter, students benefit from the type of total immersion that involvement in a one year-long program allows. Freshmen can choose among eight or ten "core" programs for first-year students. These might include "Democracy and Tyranny," "Problems Without Solutions," "Great Books," and "Reflections on Nature." Evergreen's core programs involve team teaching and incorporate multiple ways of knowing. Typically, students encounter lecture, workshops, field trips, and book seminars. There is heavy stress on various skills such as writing, speaking, library research methods, group work, self-assessment, and critical thinking.

## Respecting Diversity: The Principle in Action

Many institutions are striving to embrace diversity with great imagination and commitment. The following brief examples are drawn from both public and private institutions.

### Programs to Diversify the Student Body

Many colleges now recognize that a diverse student body is a major resource in an academic community. As a result, these institutions are actively working to increase the diversity in their student body. They usually have well-defined approaches to student recruitment, and they work hard to attract the students they regard as "good matches" for their institutions. They also seek to remove barriers to student enrollment. Admissions policies, financial aid programs, and special recruitment efforts are clear places where these efforts are evident.

- Ft. Lewis College in Colorado, University of Minnesota-Morris, and University of Maine at Farmington have special programs that allow persons of Native American heritage to register tuition-free.

  Ft. Lewis College
  Admissions Office
  Durango, CO 81301
  (303) 247-7010

  University of Minnesota-Morris
  Admissions Office
  Morris, MN 56267
  (612) 589-2211

  University of Maine at Farmington
  Admissions Office
  Farmington, ME 04938
  (207) 778-7000

### Programs to Diversify the Faculty

Most college faculties suffer from under-representation of both women and ethnic minorities. Aggressive faculty recruitment efforts are dramatically changing the faces of the faculty at many institutions.

Diversity of faculty can be cultivated in many different ways. Some colleges are working to expand the very notion of who can serve on "the faculty." For instance, many institutions use the considerable skills of retired professionals who live in the area. Retirees are used as mentors, career advisors, and participants in undergraduate research projects. Cooperative ventures with local businesses and industries have also increased the diversity of the faculty and added "real life experience" to the classroom.

Many other campuses make use of residencies and visiting

artist programs which bring professional writers, poets, dancers, and artists to campus for teaching assignments, workshops, and interaction with students.

## Responding to Student Diversity

- At the College of St. Catherine, a small liberal arts college for women with a significant number of non-traditional students, the challenge was to offer an elective, laboratory-based science course for non-science majors that would be both appealing in content and non-threatening in format. The result, "Great Ideas in Science," examines the nature of how scientists think and the processes of science so that students understand how science operates as well as its limitations, hopes, and promises.

  Terrence Flower, Department of Physics
  College of St. Catherine, P.O. Box 4084
  2004 Randolph Ave.
  St. Paul, MN 55105
  (612) 690-6203

- Recognizing that students can interpret exam questions in different ways, students in nursing courses at Georgia State University are given the opportunity to modify multiple choice exam questions that they find confusing. Student input lessens their test anxiety while allowing the students an equitable opportunity to demonstrate what they know.

  Carolyn C. Kee
  Georgia State University
  University Plaza
  Atlanta, GA 30303
  (404) 651-2000

- The diverse collection of learners in a classroom can make facilitating meaningful class discussion difficult. According to Andrew Knoedler and Mary Ann Shea, faculty can better conduct classroom discussions if they understand and apply what is known about students' cognitive development. In an article which appeared in *To Improve The Academy*, they summarized three of the cognitive theories and made specific suggestions for translating the theories into discussion techniques.

  Knoedler, A., and Shea, M. A. (1992). Conducting discussions in

the diverse classroom. *To Improve the Academy*, v. 11, 123–135.
Accommodating diverse learning styles in the classroom isn't
just the teacher's responsibility. Students need to understand their
own learning style and how to make the most of it.

- Neil D. Fleming and Colleen Mills are working on developing
  a self assessment instrument for student learning styles that is
  accompanied by a chart which offers students tips for using
  that learning style during class, while studying, and when taking exams.

   Fleming, N. D., and Mills, C. (1992). Not another inventory;
   Rather a catalyst for reflections. *To Improve the Academy*,
   Vol. 11, pp. 137–155.

### Living and Learning Options

Within a traditional college environment, alternative living
and learning options can also nurture diversity. Students' needs
may be met by allowing them to individualize their own programs
of study. Institutions may also meet students' needs through programs that create small learning communities within the larger
campus environments.

Honors programs are one learning option. Colleges such as the
University of Maryland make honors programs available to all
interested students. Others define their honors programs in traditional terms of academic excellence and are selective in admissions.

Cluster colleges offer another alternative. A number of colleges have organized living-learning centers that integrate the residential and academic experiences and build a greater sense of
community.

- The University of California at Santa Cruz is organized around
  eight cluster colleges, each with a distinctive curricular identity,
  ranging from the arts to marine studies to third world studies.

   James Quann
   Vice Chancellor of Students Affairs
   University of California at Santa Cruz
   Santa Cruz, CA 95064
   (408) 459-2474

- Western Washington University's Fairhaven College has a cluster college with an interdisciplinary curriculum and an emphasis on student-centered approaches to teaching and learning.

  Marie Eaton, Dean
  Western Washington University—Fairhaven College
  Bellingham, WA 98225-9118
  (206) 650-3680

- St. Lawrence University in New York has an established first-year student program involving residential thematic colleges.

  Dr. Grant Cornwell
  Associate Dean of First Year
  St. Lawrence University
  Canton, NY 13617
  (315) 379-5909

Many colleges and universities offer residential students the option to participate in thematic residence halls focused on a specific language, field of study, or interest.

Students of non-traditional age often require the options of flexible scheduling, independent study, and individualized programming.

- DePaul University's School for New Learning (SNL) strives to create a personalized, flexible, experiential learning environment for its non-traditional learners. Courses in the SNL can be traditional academic classes or independent study, and they focus on a competence framework rather than on specific content or credit-hour requirements. Students wishing to enter the SNL program participate in a Discovery Workshop, a pre-admission entry program. This workshop consists of a series of seminars that provide an opportunity for adults to engage in self-evaluation and educational planning as they consider returning to school.

  Douglas Murphy, Assistant Dean
  School for New Learning
  DePaul University
  25 East Jackson Blvd.
  Chicago, IL 60604
  (312) 362-8001

- The K Plan at Kalamazoo College is a system of alternative on- and off-campus study that allows students to spend significant portions of their college careers on career-development internships, foreign study, and individualized projects.

  Dr. Richard Cook, Provost
  Kalamazoo College
  1200 Academy St.
  Kalamazoo, MI 49006
  (616) 337-7162

Cross-registration options through consortia represent a way colleges and universities are responding to diverse student needs. A number of colleges have established consortia relationships which broaden students' program options. Study abroad programs are widely available through such relationships, but the model can also apply to other program areas.

- The "Five College Consortium" in central Massachusetts, which includes both private and public institutions, allows students to cross-register in courses at any of the five schools: Hampshire College, University of Massachusetts-Amherst, Smith, Amherst, and Mt. Holyoke.

  Carol Angus
  Associate Coordinator
  Five Colleges, Inc.
  97 Spring Street
  Amherst, MA 01002
  (413) 256-8316

- Students at North Dakota State University, Concordia College-Moorhead, and Moorhead State University (both in Minnesota) have the opportunity to register for classes on any of the three campuses. Unique in that the participating schools are both public and private and in two different states, the success of this program demonstrates how commitment to offering students options for a quality education can overcome numerous obstacles.

Dave Nelson, Associate Registrar
Moorhead State University
Box 411
1104 4th Avenue South
Moorhead, MN 56563
(218) 236-2581

*Russell M. Lidman is former Provost and now a member of the faculty, The Evergreen State College.*

*Barbara Leigh Smith is Academic Vice President and Provost, The Evergreen State College.*

*Thomas L. Purce is Executive Vice President for Finance and Administration, The Evergreen State College.*

### References

Hodgkinson, H. (1985). *All One System: Demographics of Education, Kindergarten Through Graduate School.* Washington, DC: Institute of Educational Leadership.

Bonnwell, C., and Eison, J. (1991). *Active Learning: Creating Excitement in the Classroom.* ERIC-ASHE Higher Education Report No. 1.

Claxton, C., & Murrell, P. (1987). *Learning Styles: Implications for Improving Educational Practices.* ERIC-ASHE Higher Education Report No. 4, 1987.

## Resources: Diverse Learning Styles

Discovering the liberal arts in an optional integrated core: Kalamazoo College. (1988). *Liberal Education, 74* (4), 30–31.

Hill, P. J. (1991). Multiculturalism: The crucial philosophical and organizational issues. *Change,* 38–47.

Jacobs, L. C., and Chase, C. I. (1992). *Developing and Using Tests Effectively: A Guide for Faculty.* San Francisco, CA: Jossey-Bass.

Kee, C. C. (1994). Multiple choice questions: A new twist for an old standard. *The Teaching Professor, 8* (6), 6.

Kolb, D. (1981). Learning styles and disciplinary differences. In *The Modern American College,* edited by A.W. Chickering and Associates. San Francisco, CA: Jossey-Bass.

Lynch, J. M., and Bishop-Clark, C. (1993). Traditional and nontra-
ditional student attitudes toward the mixed age classroom.
*Innovative Higher Education.* Winter, 109–121.

National Institute of Education. (1984). *Involvement in Learning:
Realizing the Potential of American Higher Education.* Final report
of the study group on the conditions of excellence in American
higher education. Washington, DC: U.S. Department of Education News.

Richardson, R. (1985). How are students learning? *Change,* 17 (3),
43–49.

Richardson, R. C. (1992). Improving state and campus environments for quality and diversity: A self assessment. Unpublished Report. Eric microfiche ed349914.

School for new learning provides competence based program:
DePaul University. (1988). *Liberal Education,* 74 (3), 30–32.

The limits, promises, and hopes of science: College of St. Catherine. (1988). *Liberal Education,* 74 (2), 24–25.

# 8

# INDICATORS OF EDUCATIONAL EFFECTIVENESS

*James Reynolds*

## Introduction

A wise person once observed, "Education is one of the few things a person is willing to pay for and not get." This statement speaks not only to the motivation required to obtain a high-quality education but to making the "right" choice among alternative learning environments that will actually result in the achievement of identified outcomes.

The Seven Principles—and the research base that supports them—have emerged not only as guides to structuring student and faculty interaction in the classroom, but also as a framework which suggests indicators that can be used to distinguish quality learning environments. The nation and its schools and colleges are faced with a difficult task of bringing about a level of organizational change that will result in improved educational quality, student achievement, and as a consequence, better global economic competitiveness. The changes required to achieve this goal must focus fundamentally on what takes place between student and teacher in the classroom. The Seven Principles offer not only a set of goals and a plan of action in this regard but a set of indicators that will assist in measuring progress as well.

## The Educational Environment and Indicators of Quality

In light of national and state demands for improvement in educational quality, decades of research on the effects of college have recently been given timely prominence. Two works, in particular, highlight the many impacts of higher education on students and address features of the educational environment that influence student achievement .

In their book, *How College Affects Students: Findings and Insights from Twenty Years of Research*, Pascarella and Terenzini (1991) identify the following impacts of the educational environment:

- living on campus is a critical variable to college impact so students experience other forces of change on campus

- informal, non-classroom contacts between students and faculty are responsible for increases in intellectuality, maturity, autonomy, educational aspirations/attainments, and interpersonal skills

- teaching methods that stress active learning produce a wide range of intellectual and personal effects

- the academic major influences what students know about the field

- relationships with peers, while not as influential as faculty relationships on intellectual development, are important to other areas of student maturation

Such research findings clearly suggest, according to Gamson (1991) "...that colleges that involve their students in learning and bind them socially to the collegiate environment have an impact." These findings indicate the importance of evaluating the quality of the learning environment in making choices among higher education institutions and providing indicators for assessing the quality of that environment.

The second work—and perhaps the more helpful volume because of its specific focus on the teaching and learning environment in college settings—is the work edited by Arthur Chickering and Zelda Gamson, *New Directions in Teaching and Learning: Applying the Seven Principles for Good Practice in Undergraduate Education.* Their volume makes a convincing case, based on over 50 years of research, that the practice of the Seven Principles enables the creation of an educational environment that maximizes student learning and achievement of desired outcomes.

The Seven Principles enjoy such popularity that they are now widely practiced among institutions whose primary mission is to provide high quality undergraduate instruction. Can these principles be utilized to assist in distinguishing high quality, educationally effective learning environments? What indicators, based on these principles, may be identified?

## Utilizing the Seven Principles as Guides to Evaluating the Quality of Undergraduate Education

Many people need to evaluate the quality of a higher education institution in order to make recommendations to others (or themselves). Educational leaders, political officials, foundation board members, and consumers need and want to know how to judge educational quality. The Seven Principles provide a framework for identifying indicators of quality and effectiveness in an educational environment.

Peter Ewell, Senior Associate at the National Center for Higher Education Management Systems (NCHEMS), has devoted considerable thought to identifying indicators of instructional quality based on the Seven Principles. The following identifies each principle and the indicators that consumers might use to evaluate an institution's instructional environment based, principally, on Ewell's work. Consumers should inquire and press administrators, faculty, staff, and even students to provide information on each, or at least a selection, of the following indicators. Institutions will vary in the availability of data on each of the indicators listed.

### Good Practice Encourages Student-Faculty Contact

Ample evidence indicates that frequent student-faculty contact in and outside of the classroom affects student motivation and involvement. Indicators that may be used to evaluate this feature of the educational environment include:

- overall student-faculty ratio
- average section size (excluding independent study and internships)
- percentage of sections with 15 or fewer students enrolled
- percentage of faculty who report knowing the majority of their students by name
- percentage of students involved in faculty research
- students' overall frequency of out-of-class contact with faculty
- students' opportunity for in-class discussion
- percentage of students reporting having visited faculty during established office hours
- average number of hours faculty spend advising each week
- percent of students reporting after-class conversations on academic subjects with faculty

### Good Practice Encourages Cooperation

Working with others collaboratively rather than competitively enhances learning. Indicators for evaluating the quality of cooperative learning environments include:

- percentage of faculty who report efforts to create group projects or learning communities in their classes
- percentage of courses that include team projects or similar group learning experiences
- percentage of students participating in group study
- percentage of students reporting frequent out-of-class discussions with fellow students on course content
- use of non-competitive grading techniques (competency-based, criterion-referenced vs. use of the normal curve)

### Good Practice Encourages Active Learning

Students who become involved in their learning rather than passively sitting and listening will learn more and better. Relevant indicators of quality for this principle include:

- percentage of faculty using teaching techniques that involve student's active participation

- number of internships, practica, or other practice-oriented courses offered per student
- number of independent study courses offered per student
- percentage of graduating seniors engaging in at least one internship, practicum, independent study, or similar practice-oriented course
- percentage of courses requiring students to engage in independent research papers, projects, presentations, or similar exercise
- percentage of courses requiring students to use the library as a research resource
- percentage of faculty reporting giving students credit for active class participation
- percentage of students reporting using the library as a result of a class assignment
- percentage of graduating seniors reporting opportunities for field projects in courses during their career

### Good Practice Gives Prompt Feedback

A highly effective learning environment involves students receiving frequent, timely, and appropriate feedback on their performance. Indicators in this section include:

- average number of graded assignments or exercises given per course
- average number of graded tests and quizzes per course
- average "turnaround" time for submission of final course grades
- percentage of students reporting that they generally received graded assignments back from instructors within one week
- percentage of students reporting that instructors provided frequent and specific oral comments on performance
- percentage of students reporting that the instructor systematically reviewed tests or assignments in class after papers were returned

- percentage of graduating seniors reporting that frequent instructor feedback helped improve their undergraduate performance

## Good Practice Emphasizes Time on Task

Time and energy are required for learning. There is no substitute for clear expectations regarding time management needed for effective learning. Indicators in this area include:

- average student course load taken per term

- percentage of courses with clear attendance policy

- average amount of time spent studying for class or working on assignments per week

- average number of hours per week spent on academic assignments as reported by graduating seniors

- percentage of available library spaces occupied by students from 5:00 to 9:00 p.m.

## Good Practice Communicates High Expectations

Achievement in learning is related to the level of expectations. When teachers and institutions hold high expectations, student achievement rises to meet those expectations. Several indicators of quality are evident here, and include:

- average ACT/SAT of entering freshmen

- average number of pages of reading and writing assignments in humanities and social sciences courses

- overall distribution of grades granted each term

- percentage of seniors graduating without writing a major research paper during their undergraduate career

- percentage of students reporting not being significantly challenged by class material and assignments

## Good Practice Respects Diverse Talents and Ways of Learning

Students learn in different ways and possess many abilities. A high quality learning environment is sensitive to these differences and capitalizes on them to assist students to achieve identified learning outcomes. Some indicators include:

- percentage of courses requiring students to speak in class and percentage requiring students to view visual material as part of assignments
- percentage of students reporting that they were encouraged to ask questions in class
- percentage of students reporting that the grading and evaluation process used by the instructor allowed them to actually demonstrate what they knew
- percentage of students reporting that performance evaluations permitted demonstrations of competencies in different ways
- percentage of faculty reporting that they regularly use individualized or alternative forms of instruction to communicate course materials
- percentage of faculty reporting knowledge about, and use of, formal differences in learning styles among students to organize their courses

## Conclusion

How does one distinguish a high quality educational environment? Readers are encouraged to formulate questions around a selection of the above indicators and ask them of education representatives in order to form a judgment.

However, no one indicator is sufficient to provide an accurate measure of the quality of an institution's learning environment. Multiple indicators are required to do this, and the reader is encouraged to add indicators to the list suggested here.

Choosing a high quality educational institution is a concern of many today. Making informed decisions based on indicators of educational effectiveness enhance the likelihood of consumers making the right choice.

*James Reynolds is Professor of Sociology, Winona State University.*

## References

Chickering, A. and Gamson, A., (Eds.). (1991). *New Directions in Teaching and Learning: Applying The Seven Principles for Good Practice in Undergraduate Education.* San Francisco, CA: Jossey-Bass.

Gamson, Z. (1991). Why is college so influential? *Change.* 23 (6), 50–53.

*Indicators for Improving Undergraduate Instructional Quality.* (1990). Unpublished working document commissioned by Winona State University and based on the "Seven Principles for Good Practice in Undergraduate Education."

Pascarella, P. T. and Terenzini, E. T. (1991). *How College Affects Students: Findings and Insights from Twenty Years of Research.* San Francisco, CA: Jossey-Bass.

## Resources

These works are extremely important for their cataloging of the variety of impacts higher education has on attitudes, personality, motivation, values, earnings (although not uniformly for everyone), occupational status, knowledge, cognitive development, health, and life span to mention a few.

Chickering, A. (1969). *Education and Identity.* San Francisco, CA: Jossey-Bass.

Feldman, K. & Newcomb, T. (1969). *Impact of College on Students.* San Francisco, CA: Jossey-Bass.

Solmon, L. C., and Taubman, P. J. (1973). *Does College Matter? Some Evidence on the Impacts of Higher Education.* New York, NY.: Academic Press.

Winter, et. al. *A New Case for the Liberal Arts.* (1982), San Francisco, CA: Jossey-Bass.

# 9

# INVENTORIES FOR GOOD PRACTICE IN UNDERGRADUATE EDUCATION

## Faculty and Institutional Inventories

These Inventories are designed to help faculty members, departments, colleges, and universities examine individual behaviors and institutional policies and practices for their consistency with Seven Principles for Good Practice in Undergraduate Education.

The Inventories are in two parts which can be used jointly or separately. The Faculty Inventory has seven sections, one for each Principle: Student-Faculty Contact, Cooperation Among Students, Active Learning, Prompt Feedback, Time on Task, High Expectations, and Diverse Talents and Ways of Learning. It can be useful to faculty members, student services staff, and administrators who also teach. The questions address activities consistent with Good Practice in Undergraduate Education and help respondents identify activities they might wish to pursue.

The Institutional Inventory has six sections: Climate, Academic Practices, Curriculum, Faculty, Academic and Student Support Services, and Facilities. These questions deal with various aspects of the institution as a whole. They address policies, practices, institutional norms, and expectations that support good practice. This section can be used by persons or groups associated with the institution, whether or not they teach.

These Inventories are not neutral. They express the point of view in the Principles. These Principles are anchored in decades of research about teaching, learning, and the college experience. It is obvious which responses are "good" with respect to each Principle so it is easy to create a positive picture. The Inventories will be useful only to the extent that responses are honest reports of individual behaviors and the institutional environment.

The purpose of these Inventories is the improvement of undergraduate education, not the evaluation of individual units, faculty, or administrators. The Inventories will be most helpful if they are used as a basis for diagnosis, rather than as a basis for judgment about performance, summative evaluation, or self-justification. In conjunction with the Principles statement, they can be used in a variety of ways by individuals or groups.

The Faculty Inventory can be used by faculty members who are interested in improving their own teaching, or as a basis for discussion in department meetings, curriculum committee meetings, and other committees concerned with undergraduates. This inventory will be used best by faculty members as a stimulus to becoming more effective. It can also suggest professional development activities for both faculty members and administrators.

The Institutional Inventory will be used best by institutions or by sub-units to create more educationally powerful environments. Administrators may find the Institutional Inventory useful in discussions of goals and as an aid in long-range planning.

## Student Inventory

These Inventories are designed to help students assume an active role in their learning. The Inventories may be used by students, faculty, and others in a variety of ways: in small groups, in classrooms, in one-on-one discussions or advising sessions, or in residential settings.

In whatever way they are used, it is important to remember that the content of the Inventories is not neutral. It is grounded in the Seven Principles for Good Practice in Undergraduate Education, and thus embodies decades of research about teaching, learning, and the college experience. These Inventories will be useful to the students for self analysis only to the extent that each response is an honest report of individual behavior.

The purpose of the Inventories is the improvement of undergraduate education and enhancement of the educational experience of each student, not the evaluation of individual students, instructors, or classes. The Inventories will be most helpful if they are used as a basis for diagnosis rather than judgment about performance, summative evaluation, or self-justification.

# FACULTY INVENTORY

**1  Good Practice Encourages
Student-Faculty Contact**

|  | Very Often | Often | Occasionally | Rarely | Never |
|---|---|---|---|---|---|
| 1) I advise my students about career opportunities in their major field. | ☐ | ☐ | ☐ | ☐ | ☐ |
| 2) Students drop by my office just to visit. | ☐ | ☐ | ☐ | ☐ | ☐ |
| 3) I share my past experiences, attitudes, and values with students. | ☐ | ☐ | ☐ | ☐ | ☐ |
| 4) I attend events sponsored by student groups. | ☐ | ☐ | ☐ | ☐ | ☐ |
| 5) I work with student affairs staff on issues related to student extracurricular life and life outside of school. | ☐ | ☐ | ☐ | ☐ | ☐ |
| 6) I know my students by name by the end of the first two weeks of the term. | ☐ | ☐ | ☐ | ☐ | ☐ |
| 7) I make special efforts to be available to students of a culture or race different from my own. | ☐ | ☐ | ☐ | ☐ | ☐ |
| 8) I serve as a mentor or informal advisor to students. | ☐ | ☐ | ☐ | ☐ | ☐ |
| 9) I take students to professional meetings or other events in my field. | ☐ | ☐ | ☐ | ☐ | ☐ |
| 10) Whenever there is a conflict on campus involving students, I try to help in its resolution. | ☐ | ☐ | ☐ | ☐ | ☐ |

As I look at my responses to this section, I would like to work on:

## 2   Good Practice Encourages Cooperation Among Students

| | Very Often | Often | Occasionally | Rarely | Never |
|---|:---:|:---:|:---:|:---:|:---:|
| 1) I ask students to tell each other about their interests and backgrounds. | ☐ | ☐ | ☐ | ☐ | ☐ |
| 2) I encourage my students to prepare together for classes or exams. | ☐ | ☐ | ☐ | ☐ | ☐ |
| 3) I encourage students to do projects together. | ☐ | ☐ | ☐ | ☐ | ☐ |
| 4) I ask my students to evaluate each other's work. | ☐ | ☐ | ☐ | ☐ | ☐ |
| 5) I ask my students to explain difficult ideas to each other. | ☐ | ☐ | ☐ | ☐ | ☐ |
| 6) I encourage my students to praise each other for their accomplishments. | ☐ | ☐ | ☐ | ☐ | ☐ |
| 7) I ask my students to discuss key concepts with other students whose backgrounds and viewpoints are different from their own. | ☐ | ☐ | ☐ | ☐ | ☐ |
| 8) I create "learning communities," study groups, or project teams within my courses. | ☐ | ☐ | ☐ | ☐ | ☐ |
| 9) I encourage students to join at least one campus organization. | ☐ | ☐ | ☐ | ☐ | ☐ |
| 10) I distribute performance criteria to students so that each person's grade is independent of those achieved by others. | ☐ | ☐ | ☐ | ☐ | ☐ |

As I look at my responses to this section, I would like to work on:

**3   Good Practice Encourages
     Active Learning**

| | Very Often | Often | Occasionally | Rarely | Never |
|---|---|---|---|---|---|
| 1) I ask my students to present their work to the class. | ☐ | ☐ | ☐ | ☐ | ☐ |
| 2) I ask my students to summarize similarities and differences among different theorists, research findings, or artistic works. | ☐ | ☐ | ☐ | ☐ | ☐ |
| 3) I ask my students to relate outside events or activities to the subjects covered in my courses. | ☐ | ☐ | ☐ | ☐ | ☐ |
| 4) I ask my students to undertake research or independent study. | ☐ | ☐ | ☐ | ☐ | ☐ |
| 5) I encourage students to challenge my ideas, the ideas of other students, or those presented in readings or other course materials. | ☐ | ☐ | ☐ | ☐ | ☐ |
| 6) I give my students concrete, real-life situations to analyze. | ☐ | ☐ | ☐ | ☐ | ☐ |
| 7) I use simulations, role-playing, or labs in my classes. | ☐ | ☐ | ☐ | ☐ | ☐ |
| 8) I encourage my students to suggest new readings, research projects, field trips, or other course activities. | ☐ | ☐ | ☐ | ☐ | ☐ |
| 9) My students and I arrange field trips, volunteer activities, or internships related to the course. | ☐ | ☐ | ☐ | ☐ | ☐ |
| 10) I carry out research projects with my students. | ☐ | ☐ | ☐ | ☐ | ☐ |

As I look at my responses to this section, I would like to work on:

## 4   Good Practice Gives Prompt Feedback

|  | Very Often | Often | Occasionally | Rarely | Never |
|---|---|---|---|---|---|
| 1) I give quizzes and homework assignments. | ☐ | ☐ | ☐ | ☐ | ☐ |
| 2) I prepare classroom exercises and problems which give students immediate feedback on how well they do. | ☐ | ☐ | ☐ | ☐ | ☐ |
| 3) I return examinations and papers within a week. | ☐ | ☐ | ☐ | ☐ | ☐ |
| 4) I give students detailed evaluations of their work early in the term. | ☐ | ☐ | ☐ | ☐ | ☐ |
| 5) I ask my students to schedule conferences with me to discuss their progress. | ☐ | ☐ | ☐ | ☐ | ☐ |
| 6) I give my students written comments on their strengths and weaknesses on exams and papers. | ☐ | ☐ | ☐ | ☐ | ☐ |
| 7) I give my students a pre-test at the beginning of each course. | ☐ | ☐ | ☐ | ☐ | ☐ |
| 8) I ask students to keep logs or records of their progress. | ☐ | ☐ | ☐ | ☐ | ☐ |
| 9) I discuss the results of the final examination with my students at the end of the semester. | ☐ | ☐ | ☐ | ☐ | ☐ |
| 10) I call or write a note to students who miss classes. | ☐ | ☐ | ☐ | ☐ | ☐ |

As I look at my responses to this section, I would like to work on:

**5    Good Practice Emphasizes
Time on Task**

|  | Very Often | Often | Occasionally | Rarely | Never |
|---|---|---|---|---|---|
| 1) I expect my students to complete their assignments promptly. | ☐ | ☐ | ☐ | ☐ | ☐ |
| 2) I clearly communicate to my students the minimum amount of time they should spend preparing for classes. | ☐ | ☐ | ☐ | ☐ | ☐ |
| 3) I make clear to my students the amount of time that is required to understand complex material. | ☐ | ☐ | ☐ | ☐ | ☐ |
| 4) I help students set challenging goals for their own learning. | ☐ | ☐ | ☐ | ☐ | ☐ |
| 5) When oral reports or class presentations are called for I encourage students to rehearse in advance. | ☐ | ☐ | ☐ | ☐ | ☐ |
| 6) I underscore the importance of regular work, steady application, sound self-pacing, and scheduling. | ☐ | ☐ | ☐ | ☐ | ☐ |
| 7) I explain to my students the consequences of non-attendance. | ☐ | ☐ | ☐ | ☐ | ☐ |
| 8) I make it clear that full-time study is a full-time job that requires forty or more hours a week. | ☐ | ☐ | ☐ | ☐ | ☐ |
| 9) I meet with students who fall behind to discuss their study habits, schedules, and other commitments. | ☐ | ☐ | ☐ | ☐ | ☐ |
| 10) If students miss my classes, I require them to make up lost work. | ☐ | ☐ | ☐ | ☐ | ☐ |

As I look at my responses to this section, I would like to work on:

**6  Good Practice Communicates High Expectations**

|  | Very Often | Often | Occasionally | Rarely | Never |
|---|---|---|---|---|---|
| 1) I tell students that I expect them to work hard in my classes. | ☐ | ☐ | ☐ | ☐ | ☐ |
| 2) I emphasize the importance of holding high standards for academic achievement. | ☐ | ☐ | ☐ | ☐ | ☐ |
| 3) I make clear my expectations orally and in writing at the beginning of each course. | ☐ | ☐ | ☐ | ☐ | ☐ |
| 4) I help students set challenging goals for their own learning. | ☐ | ☐ | ☐ | ☐ | ☐ |
| 5) I explain to students what will happen if they do not complete their work on time. | ☐ | ☐ | ☐ | ☐ | ☐ |
| 6) I suggest extra reading or writing tasks. | ☐ | ☐ | ☐ | ☐ | ☐ |
| 7) I encourage students to write a lot. | ☐ | ☐ | ☐ | ☐ | ☐ |
| 8) I publicly call attention to excellent performance by my students. | ☐ | ☐ | ☐ | ☐ | ☐ |
| 9) I revise my courses. | ☐ | ☐ | ☐ | ☐ | ☐ |
| 10) I periodically discuss how well we are doing during the course of the semester. | ☐ | ☐ | ☐ | ☐ | ☐ |

As I look at my responses to this section, I would like to work on:

## 7  Good Practice Respects Diverse Talents and Ways of Learning

Very Often / Often / Occasionally / Rarely / Never

1) I encourage students to speak up when they don't understand. ☐ ☐ ☐ ☐ ☐

2) I discourage snide remarks, sarcasm, kidding, and other class behaviors that may embarrass students. ☐ ☐ ☐ ☐ ☐

3) I use diverse teaching activities to address a broad spectrum of students. ☐ ☐ ☐ ☐ ☐

4) I select readings and design activities related to the background of my students. ☐ ☐ ☐ ☐ ☐

5) I provide extra material or exercises for students who lack essential background knowledge or skills. ☐ ☐ ☐ ☐ ☐

6) I integrate new knowledge about women and other underrepresented populations into my courses. ☐ ☐ ☐ ☐ ☐

7) I make explicit provisions for students who wish to carry out independent studies within my own course or as separate courses. ☐ ☐ ☐ ☐ ☐

8) I have developed mastery learning, learning contracts, or computer assisted learning alternatives for my courses. ☐ ☐ ☐ ☐ ☐

9) I encourage my students to design their own majors when their interests warrant doing so. ☐ ☐ ☐ ☐ ☐

10) I try to find out about my students' learning styles, interests, or backgrounds at the beginning of each course. ☐ ☐ ☐ ☐ ☐

As I look at my responses to this section, I would like to work on:

## Summary Responses

After reviewing my responses to these seven areas and the items within them, the key area(s) I would like to work on is/are:

The people or groups in the best position to act on these items are:

# INSTITUTIONAL INVENTORY

## 1   Climate

*Very Often    Often    Occasionally    Rarely    Never*

1) There are functions on campus when students and faculty get together informally. ☐ ☐ ☐ ☐ ☐

2) There is student representation on major faculty and administrative committees. ☐ ☐ ☐ ☐ ☐

3) Students are publicly recognized for superior academic performance. ☐ ☐ ☐ ☐ ☐

4) This institution successfully recruits and retains minority faculty, staff, and students. ☐ ☐ ☐ ☐ ☐

5) Senior administrators explicitly recognize faculty and student contributions to institutional policies and practices. ☐ ☐ ☐ ☐ ☐

6) Institutional publications reflect diversity in the student body, faculty, and staff. ☐ ☐ ☐ ☐ ☐

7) The administration encourages faculty to hold high expectations for student performance. ☐ ☐ ☐ ☐ ☐

8) The President and other senior administrators are accessible to faculty members and students. ☐ ☐ ☐ ☐ ☐

9) Faculty members and administrators go out of their way to create a hospitable climate on campus. ☐ ☐ ☐ ☐ ☐

10) Senior administrators, deans, and department heads set examples of collaborative relationships. ☐ ☐ ☐ ☐ ☐

11) Students know that people work hard on this campus. ☐ ☐ ☐ ☐ ☐

As I look at my responses to this section, I think my institution should work on:

The people or groups in the best position to act on these items are:

| | Very Often | Often | Occasionally | Rarely | Never |
|---|---|---|---|---|---|
| **2  Academic Practices** | | | | | |
| 1) Students may test out of requirements they have already met or subjects they know. | ☐ | ☐ | ☐ | ☐ | ☐ |
| 2) This institution speaks to relationships between the course load students assume and other responsibilities such as work, family, and community activities. | ☐ | ☐ | ☐ | ☐ | ☐ |
| 3) This institution compares salary levels for male and female staff. | ☐ | ☐ | ☐ | ☐ | ☐ |
| 4) This institution keeps track of how its graduates are doing. | ☐ | ☐ | ☐ | ☐ | ☐ |
| 5) Students are given opportunities to evaluate academic programs and suggest changes. | ☐ | ☐ | ☐ | ☐ | ☐ |
| 6) This institution imposes limitations on the number of incompletes students can carry. | ☐ | ☐ | ☐ | ☐ | ☐ |
| 7) Faculty members articulate clear criteria for evaluating students' work. | ☐ | ☐ | ☐ | ☐ | ☐ |
| 8) This institution sends reports to students on their progress in meeting requirements. | ☐ | ☐ | ☐ | ☐ | ☐ |
| 9) Part-time faculty play other important roles besides teaching their courses. | ☐ | ☐ | ☐ | ☐ | ☐ |
| 10) This institution assesses changes in student knowledge and competence during their attendance. | ☐ | ☐ | ☐ | ☐ | ☐ |
| 11) Athletes are held to the same academic expectations as other students. | ☐ | ☐ | ☐ | ☐ | ☐ |

As I look at my responses to this section, I think my institution should work on:

The people or groups in the best position to act on these items are:

**3 Curriculum**

|  | Very Often | Often | Occasionally | Rarely | Never |
|---|---|---|---|---|---|
| 1) Courses incorporate field experiences or hands-on applications. | ☐ | ☐ | ☐ | ☐ | ☐ |
| 2) Faculty revise and monitor the general education requirements. | ☐ | ☐ | ☐ | ☐ | ☐ |
| 3) Faculty revise and monitor requirements in the major. | ☐ | ☐ | ☐ | ☐ | ☐ |
| 4) Students engage in independent study, contract-learning, or mastery learning. | ☐ | ☐ | ☐ | ☐ | ☐ |
| 5) Freshmen enroll in special programs. | ☐ | ☐ | ☐ | ☐ | ☐ |
| 6) Students participate in a cooperative work program or an internship program. | ☐ | ☐ | ☐ | ☐ | ☐ |
| 7) Faculty and students are aware of the knowledge, skills, and attitudes this institution expects its students to develop by the time they graduate. | ☐ | ☐ | ☐ | ☐ | ☐ |
| 8) Students pursue their own individually designed majors. | ☐ | ☐ | ☐ | ☐ | ☐ |
| 9) Students enroll in interdisciplinary majors. | ☐ | ☐ | ☐ | ☐ | ☐ |
| 10) Students participate in programs which help them appreciate cultural diversity. | ☐ | ☐ | ☐ | ☐ | ☐ |
| 11) Students enroll in learning communities, cluster courses, or special seminars designed to help them see relationships among the subjects they study. | ☐ | ☐ | ☐ | ☐ | ☐ |

As I look at my responses to this section, I think my institution should work on:

The people or groups in the best position to act on these items are:

| | Very Often | Often | Occasionally | Rarely | Never |
|---|---|---|---|---|---|
| **4   Faculty** | | | | | |
| 1) Faculty members are on campus and available to students during the week. | ☐ | ☐ | ☐ | ☐ | ☐ |
| 2) Explicit criteria are used for evaluating teaching performance. | ☐ | ☐ | ☐ | ☐ | ☐ |
| 3) Faculty members receive feedback concerning their performance as teachers and advisors. | ☐ | ☐ | ☐ | ☐ | ☐ |
| 5) Limits on outside consulting and other private ventures are discussed with faculty members. | ☐ | ☐ | ☐ | ☐ | ☐ |
| 6) Faculty take academic advising seriously. | ☐ | ☐ | ☐ | ☐ | ☐ |
| 7) Annual merit increases are directly tied to faculty performance in teaching. | ☐ | ☐ | ☐ | ☐ | ☐ |
| 8) Faculty members work with student services staff members. | ☐ | ☐ | ☐ | ☐ | ☐ |
| 9) This institution recognizes advising as a legitimate part of the faculty's work load. | ☐ | ☐ | ☐ | ☐ | ☐ |
| 10) Faculty participate in key institutional decisions, such as those concerned with long range planning, budget, and personnel. | ☐ | ☐ | ☐ | ☐ | ☐ |
| 11) Faculty evaluate administrators' contributions to the educational climate of this institution. | ☐ | ☐ | ☐ | ☐ | ☐ |

As I look at my responses to this section, I think my institution should work on:

The people or groups in the best position to act on these items are:

**5   Academic and Student
     Support Services**

Very Often · Often · Occasionally · Rarely · Never

1) Counseling services address a wide
   range of student concerns.              ☐ ☐ ☐ ☐ ☐

2) Students go to a writing laboratory for
   help with papers and writing
   problems.                               ☐ ☐ ☐ ☐ ☐

3) Time management seminars are
   offered to students.                    ☐ ☐ ☐ ☐ ☐

4) Students with poor academic
   preparation receive help in improving
   their academic skills.                  ☐ ☐ ☐ ☐ ☐

5) Student Affairs, Academic Affairs, and
   the Student Government jointly carry
   out the orientation program.            ☐ ☐ ☐ ☐ ☐

6) Students serve as tutors, advisors, or
   resource persons for other students.    ☐ ☐ ☐ ☐ ☐

7) Students receive professional
   assistance in preparing their financial
   aid forms.                              ☐ ☐ ☐ ☐ ☐

8) Educational objectives are specified
   for student activities.                 ☐ ☐ ☐ ☐ ☐

9) Students work with the same advisor
   during the entire period of their
   enrollment.                             ☐ ☐ ☐ ☐ ☐

10) This institution trains faculty, staff,
    and students to deal with student
    diversity.                             ☐ ☐ ☐ ☐ ☐

11) Financial aid checks are available for
    distribution on the first day of classes
    for those who apply by the deadline.   ☐ ☐ ☐ ☐ ☐

As I look at my responses to this section, I think my institution should
work on:


The people or groups in the best position to act on these items are:

| | Very Often | Often | Occasionally | Rarely | Never |
|---|---|---|---|---|---|
| **6  Facilities** | | | | | |
| 1) Classrooms have moveable furniture. | ☐ | ☐ | ☐ | ☐ | ☐ |
| 2) Comfortable places where students can meet with faculty are available. | ☐ | ☐ | ☐ | ☐ | ☐ |
| 3) Study spaces conducive to quiet concentration are available. | ☐ | ☐ | ☐ | ☐ | ☐ |
| 4) Recreational and athletic facilities are open evenings and weekends. | ☐ | ☐ | ☐ | ☐ | ☐ |
| 5) A cafeteria, snack bar, or other eating facility is open during the day and evening. | ☐ | ☐ | ☐ | ☐ | ☐ |
| 6) Students use video, laboratory, and artistic equipment on campus. | ☐ | ☐ | ☐ | ☐ | ☐ |
| 7) Students use computers provided by the university. | ☐ | ☐ | ☐ | ☐ | ☐ |
| 8) Parking facilities adequate to serve the needs of students, faculty, and staff are available. | ☐ | ☐ | ☐ | ☐ | ☐ |
| 9) Public transportation to and from the campus is available to students during the day and evening. | ☐ | ☐ | ☐ | ☐ | ☐ |
| 10) Over the course of the semester, the library is open late evenings and weekends. | ☐ | ☐ | ☐ | ☐ | ☐ |
| 11) Administrative and Student Services offices are open for students who take courses at night. | ☐ | ☐ | ☐ | ☐ | ☐ |

As I look at my responses to this section, I think my institution should work on:

The people or groups in the best position to act on these items are:

**Summary Responses**

After reviewing my responses to these six items and the items within them, I think the most important area(s) for my institution to work on is/are:

The people or groups in the best position to act on these items are:

## STUDENT INVENTORY

**1    Student-Faculty Contact**

|  | Very Often | Often | Occasionally | Rarely | Never |
|---|---|---|---|---|---|
| 1) I look for opportunities to develop informal relationships with one or more of my professors. | ☐ | ☐ | ☐ | ☐ | ☐ |
| 2) I seek feedback from my professors about my work. | ☐ | ☐ | ☐ | ☐ | ☐ |
| 3) I question my professors when I disagree with what is said. | ☐ | ☐ | ☐ | ☐ | ☐ |
| 4) I talk with my professors outside of class about my courses and other things. | ☐ | ☐ | ☐ | ☐ | ☐ |
| 5) I find out about my professors - what else they teach, areas of expertise, and other areas of interest. | ☐ | ☐ | ☐ | ☐ | ☐ |
| 6) I attend events in which faculty are involved. | ☐ | ☐ | ☐ | ☐ | ☐ |
| 7) I give my professors feedback about the courses in which I am enrolled. | ☐ | ☐ | ☐ | ☐ | ☐ |

As I look at my responses to this section, I think I should work on:

The people or groups in the best position to help me improve on these items are:

|  | Very Often | Often | Occasionally | Rarely | Never |
|---|---|---|---|---|---|

## 2   Cooperation Among Students

1) I try to get to know my classmates. ☐ ☐ ☐ ☐ ☐

2) I study with other students in my courses. ☐ ☐ ☐ ☐ ☐

3) I work with other students in informal groups. ☐ ☐ ☐ ☐ ☐

4) I assist other students when they ask me for help. ☐ ☐ ☐ ☐ ☐

5) I tell other students when I think they have done good work. ☐ ☐ ☐ ☐ ☐

6) I discuss issues with students whose background and viewpoint differ from mine. ☐ ☐ ☐ ☐ ☐

7) I offer to serve as tutor, advisor or resource person when I am knowledgeable and can share skills with others. ☐ ☐ ☐ ☐ ☐

As I look at my responses to this section, I think I should work on:

The people or groups in the best position to help me improve on these items are:

3   **Active Learning**

1) I speak up when I don't
   understand class material.            ☐  ☐  ☐  ☐  ☐

2) I question the assumptions
   of the materials in my
   courses.                             ☐  ☐  ☐  ☐  ☐

3) I try to relate outside events
   or activities to the subjects
   covered in my courses.               ☐  ☐  ☐  ☐  ☐

4) I seek real world
   experiences to supplement
   my courses.                          ☐  ☐  ☐  ☐  ☐

5) I carefully assess my
   preparation and back-
   ground for the courses
   I take.                              ☐  ☐  ☐  ☐  ☐

6) I seek out new readings
   and/or research projects
   related to my courses.               ☐  ☐  ☐  ☐  ☐

7) I take careful notes in
   my classes.                          ☐  ☐  ☐  ☐  ☐

As I look at my responses to this section, I think I should work on:

The people or groups in the best position to help me improve on these items are:

| | Very Often | Often | Occasionally | Rarely | Never |
|---|---|---|---|---|---|

**4    Prompt Feedback**

1) When I get feedback from my professors on exams, papers, or other class work, I review their responses to assess my strengths and weaknesses.  □ □ □ □ □

2) I talk over feedback with my professors as soon as possible if anything is not clear.  □ □ □ □ □

3) I re-draft my papers and seek feedback from the professor in doing so.  □ □ □ □ □

4) I list my questions that I have from my class or my readings and follow them up by consulting with peers, my professor, or on my own.  □ □ □ □ □

5) I consider feedback from peers and then consciously decide how to act on it.  □ □ □ □ □

6) I keep a journal in which I reflect on what I am learning.  □ □ □ □ □

7) I think about what I am learning from my courses and discuss it with my professors.  □ □ □ □ □

As I look at my responses to this section, I think I should work on:

The people or groups in the best position to help me improve on these items are:

## 5    Time on Task

|  | Very Often | Often | Occasionally | Rarely | Never |
|---|---|---|---|---|---|
| 1) I complete my assignments promptly and accurately. | ☐ | ☐ | ☐ | ☐ | ☐ |
| 2) I proofread and review my work before handing in my assignments. | ☐ | ☐ | ☐ | ☐ | ☐ |
| 3) I practice class presentations before giving them in class. | ☐ | ☐ | ☐ | ☐ | ☐ |
| 4) I maintain a regular study schedule to keep up with my classes. | ☐ | ☐ | ☐ | ☐ | ☐ |
| 5) I attend classes on a regular basis. | ☐ | ☐ | ☐ | ☐ | ☐ |
| 6) I confer with my professor if I am concerned about keeping up with a particular class. | ☐ | ☐ | ☐ | ☐ | ☐ |
| 7) I identify areas where I am weak and seek extra help to strengthen them. | ☐ | ☐ | ☐ | ☐ | ☐ |

As I look at my responses to this section, I think I should work on:



The people or groups in the best position to help me improve on these items are:

**6   High Expectations**

Very Often · Often · Occasionally · Rarely · Never

1) I set personal goals for learning in my courses.   ☐ ☐ ☐ ☐ ☐

2) I try to get clear information about my instructors' goals.   ☐ ☐ ☐ ☐ ☐

3) I keep an open mind about material, even if it is not directly related to my major or career interest.   ☐ ☐ ☐ ☐ ☐

4) I do additional unassigned work to reach my learning goals.   ☐ ☐ ☐ ☐ ☐

5) I consciously think about the trade-offs between the things I do to learn and the things I do to achieve a grade.   ☐ ☐ ☐ ☐ ☐

6) I try to achieve my very best in each class.   ☐ ☐ ☐ ☐ ☐

7) I use all the resources on campus that are pertinent to my courses.   ☐ ☐ ☐ ☐ ☐

As I look at my responses to this section, I think I should work on:

The people or groups in the best position to help me improve on these items are:

## 7   Diverse Talents and Ways of Learning

| | Very Often | Often | Occasionally | Rarely | Never |
|---|---|---|---|---|---|
| 1) I try not to embarrass other students. | ☐ | ☐ | ☐ | ☐ | ☐ |
| 2) I consciously adjust my learning style to adjust to the teaching practices of my professors. | ☐ | ☐ | ☐ | ☐ | ☐ |
| 3) I share information about myself and how I learn most effectively. | ☐ | ☐ | ☐ | ☐ | ☐ |
| 4) I show respect to students with different backgrounds and levels of learning. | ☐ | ☐ | ☐ | ☐ | ☐ |
| 5) I support my professors when they include in the content of their courses the contributions or interests of under-represented populations. | ☐ | ☐ | ☐ | ☐ | ☐ |
| 6) I try to make others aware when I see or hear sexist, racist, or otherwise offensive language or behavior. | ☐ | ☐ | ☐ | ☐ | ☐ |
| 7) I am open to considering ideas that are different than mine. | ☐ | ☐ | ☐ | ☐ | ☐ |

As I look at my responses to this section, I think I should work on:

The people or groups in the best position to help me improve on these items are:

## Summary Information

1) Outside of class, how many hours in an average week do I study or otherwise prepare for all my classes?

   A. Over 20 hours   B. 16-20   C. 11-15   D. 6-10   E. 0-5

2) Compared with other college students, how important is it for me to be successful academically?

   A. much more important      B. somewhat more
   C. about equally      D. somewhat less
   E. much less important

| | Very Much | Quite a Bit | Some | Very Little |
|---|---|---|---|---|
| 3) Learn on my own. | ☐ | ☐ | ☐ | ☐ |
| 4) Find information I need. | ☐ | ☐ | ☐ | ☐ |
| 5) Integrate ideas from various sources. | ☐ | ☐ | ☐ | ☐ |
| 6) Explain information to others. | ☐ | ☐ | ☐ | ☐ |

# 10

## HOW TO CHOOSE A COLLEGE
### *For College-Bound Students & Families*

*Martin Nemko*

### Introduction

Why this section in a book for higher educators? Native Americans tell us to walk a mile in another's moccasins. If we view college from the student's perspective, we can perhaps be more responsive to their needs. Another reason for this section is that as higher educators, we are frequently asked to assist friends and relatives in selecting a college. Finally, many of us are parents and find that helping our children to choose a college is no mean task.

College shoppers should compare institutions on how well they embody key criteria such as the Seven Principles for Good Practice in Undergraduate Education. This section provides concrete guidance on how to make that comparison.

### How To Choose A College In Two Steps

Even though colleges and universities profoundly affect a student's life, most families choose their cars with more care. But colleges vary, and a good choice can enable students to blossom. A poor choice can make them wilt, as evidenced by the fact that fewer than half of freshmen ever graduate.This section presents a way to choose well by demonstrating:

1. How to narrow from the nation's 3,400 colleges to a few best-fits.

2. How to evaluate those few colleges using the Seven Principles for Good Practice in Undergraduate Education and other important criteria. A campus visit is a key part of that evaluation, but making a useful visit is trickier than it might seem. So, a section is provided: How to Test Drive a College.

## Step 1: How to Narrow from 3,400 Colleges to a Few Top Choices

With 3,400 colleges and universities in the U.S., how can you find the best fits? It seems impossible, so most college shoppers start with a short list of familiar names. The problem is that these lists may exclude colleges at which a student might be happier, more successful, and perhaps save money. Fortunately, there's an easy yet valid way to consider all 3,400 colleges to find a handful of best-fits. Start by answering the following questions. Mark all acceptable choices.

1. *I will consider colleges with an annual total cost of:*

   *A) $30,000    B) $15,000    C) $7,000*

   Middle-income families should think especially hard about this item because they would find an expensive college burdensome yet qualify for little financial aid. Middle incomers can take solace in the excellent but lower cost institutions—for example, private institutions like Rice, Southwestern, and Hendrix and public institutions like Evergreen, Miami (OH), and Minnesota-Morris. Low-income families should consider colleges in all price ranges because, thanks to financial aid, they'll often pay little, even at the most expensive colleges.

2. *I will consider colleges with admission standards that are:*

   *A) most difficult      B) very difficult      C) moderately difficult*
   *D) minimally difficult*

   The quality of the student body affects the college experience more than any other factor. It affects the level of instruction, the caliber of discussions in and outside the classroom, the atmosphere in the residence halls, and the diploma's value in the eyes of employers and graduate schools. But before answering this item, ask yourself, "Will you be better off as a lesser light among the best and brightest or would you rather shine in less distinguished company?" Many students automatically choose the most difficult school in which they can gain admission. This is sometimes the wrong choice.

   Examples of colleges with "most difficult" admission standards are Stanford, Princeton, Williams, Pomona, Chicago, and Berkeley. The typical admitted student has an A average, an S.A.T. score of 1250–1400, and impressive extracurricular activities (for example, editor-in-chief of the high school newspaper). However, admission standards may be less rigorous if you have a desirable characteristic, for example, you're a terrific musician, athlete, child of an alum, or a member of an under-represented population.

Colleges with "very difficult" admission standards include New College of the University of South Florida, Reed, and St. John's (MD, NM). The average student has an A- average, 1100–1300 SAT scores and impressive extracurriculars.

Colleges with "moderate" admission standards include most state institutions. The average in-state student (standards are higher for out-of-staters) has B+ grades and 900–1100 SAT scores.

Colleges with minimally selective admission standards include many private four-year colleges and nearly all two-year colleges. Some accept virtually all high school graduates.

3. *I will consider colleges with a name that is:*

   *A) a brand name (e.g., Rutgers)    B) less well known (e.g., Ramapo)*

A "name" school builds many students' self-esteem. It may feel better to tell others that you attend University of Maryland than St. Mary's College of Maryland, even though for many good students, St. Mary's may be a better choice.

A "name" school may make it easier to get that first job or to be accepted into graduate school, but it doesn't provide as big an advantage as is commonly believed. For example two-thirds of students admitted to Harvard Law School come from public colleges. An American Economics Association study of 2,500 high school graduates found that career success depended more on college grades, rigor of courses taken, and extracurricular involvement than on the prestige of the institution attended. A Standard & Poor's study looked at where the nation's top executives earned their undergraduate degrees. Although Harvard and Yale came in second and third, the top producer of high-level executives was the City University of New York.

4. *I will consider colleges in a location:*

   *A) more than a two-hour drive from home    B) more than a one-day drive from home    C) other (specify):*

If you're not getting along with your parents, you may want to go to college in Timbuktu. But nationwide 85% of students attend college within a day's drive from home. Especially during the first year or two at college, and especially if you might get homesick, it feels good to have the option of going home for a weekend. Another advantage is the lower travel costs of nearby colleges. On the other hand, attending a faraway college can be exciting, exposing you to a different culture.

5. *I will consider colleges that are:*

   *A) large (10,000+)   B) medium (3,000–10,000)    C) small (below 3,000)*

   Large colleges frighten many students. After all, just going away to college is a big change. Going to a college ten times as big as a high school can be downright scary. Small colleges also appeal because classes and bureaucracy tend to be smaller while personal attention is greater. Small colleges are particularly good for students who could use a watchful eye. Many small colleges offer a strong sense of community, which even extends after graduation. Successful alumni of small colleges often go out of their way to help new graduates find employment.

   For some students, however, the appeals of a small college eventually wither: you've run out of people to meet, everyone knows your business, and you've taken courses from nearly every good professor. At a large college, there's a nearly endless supply of courses, majors, things to do, and people to meet. Facilities tend to be more extensive and football and basketball games and cultural events better attended. Many students at large institutions enjoy feeling like part of something big and famous.

6. *I will consider colleges in a setting that is:*

   *A) urban/suburban    B) rural*

   Urban means there's plenty to do: malls with seven-screen movie theaters, museums, a wide choice of restaurants, pro sports teams, abundant internship opportunities. But urban also means that students and professors may vacate campus after class, which can reduce the sense of campus community. Urban also can mean higher crime. Many rural schools make extra efforts to ensure that there are plenty of after-class activities on campus: concerts, speakers, movies, etc.

7. *I will consider colleges at which the prevailing values among students are:*

   *A) conservative    B) middle-of-the road    C) liberal*

   At conservative colleges, most students may have "traditional" goals and values. The conservative tone set by the institution may not encourage behaviors or pursuits outside of a well-defined code.

Middle-of-the-road colleges don't obviously embrace or promote particular attitudes or philosophies. There will probably be a wide range of beliefs among faculty and students, and the institution doesn't align itself with a specific constituency.

Liberal colleges may encourage a change-the-world spirit. Just as the conservative institution may favor an accepted code of values that is grounded in tradition, the liberal institution promotes challenges to traditional ideas and beliefs.

8. *I will consider colleges at which most students:*

   *A) live on or near campus 7 days a week    B) live on campus but leave most weekends    C) commute*

   A residential college allows you to use college as the halfway house between the protection of childhood and the independence of adulthood. It also affords a fuller college experience. A college to which most students commute may feel like an extension of high school, especially if you only go there to take classes and don't participate in other student activities. However, a commuter college makes more sense if you must live at home for economic or personal reasons, or have limited interest in participating in campus life. Many adults happily attend commuter colleges.

### Finding Your Top-Choice Colleges

Show your counselor your answers to the above eight questions. If you don't have a counselor, use your answers to help you sift through a college guide like *The Best 286 Colleges, Barron's Top 50, The Fiske Guide to Colleges* or *How to Get an Ivy League Education at a State University* to find colleges that meet your requirements. Share your answers with teachers, your parents and their friends, and your friends. All can provide helpful advice. Or use your answers to help you use a college-finder computer program, available at many high schools.

Once you have a manageable list of colleges which meet your basic requirements, you have to figure out how good each of these schools is. It would be terrific if a book existed that provided all this for you, but while many college guides exist, none really does a good job of assessing the *quality* of the experience provided by each institution. You'll have to do the research on your own, but the College Report Card on the next pages will help you.

Yes, this takes effort. But remember that choosing a college means deciding where you're going to spend thousands of dollars and the next 4–6 years of your life. Also remember that nationwide fewer than 40% of incoming freshmen graduate. A sound choice can boost your chances of success and happiness.

## Step 2: The College Report Card

*A tool for choosing from among your top-choice colleges*
*(also a self-assessment tool for colleges)*

Educators have identified Seven Principles for Good Practice in Undergraduate Education:

1. *Student-faculty contact*, in and out of the classroom. For example, how many hours a week are faculty typically available to see undergraduate students?

2. Opportunities for *cooperative learning*. For example, opportunities to work in groups

3. Emphasis on *active learning*. For example, discussions, simulations, debates, and projects, as opposed to courses dominated by lecture and exams requiring mere regurgitation

4. *Prompt feedback* on student work, especially when that feedback is extensive rather than just a letter grade and a brief comment

5. Emphasizing *time on task*. For example, are instructors concerned with *effective* use of time?

6. *High expectations*. For example, are students encouraged to have high aspirations, goals, and performance?

7. *Respects diverse talents and ways of learning*. For example, do most courses give students options for meeting requirements?

Based on the Seven Principles and other keys to a happy and rewarding college experience, the College Report Card on the following pages lists specific things to look for in a college.

### Directions

1. Pick approximately 10 of the 48 items on the College Report Card that you believe are most likely to affect your success and happiness at college. Put a checkmark next to these ten.

2. Make a copy of the College Report Card for each college you're considering.

3. Learn how each college measures up on the 10 College Report Card items you selected and write what you learn in the margins of the Report Card. How will you figure out what to write? By reading commercial college guides and material from the colleges, by talking with your counselor and college students home from vacation, by asking questions at college nights, by making campus visits, and by phoning college personnel and students. You can get information on many of the Report Card items by phone. For example, to talk with

students, call the college's switchboard (the phone numbers are available from directory assistance) and have the call transferred to a residence hall front desk, the student newspaper office, or the student government office.

4. By spring of your senior year, you'll have recorded quite a bit on your Report Cards. Compare the Report Cards and choose your college based on which one will best support your intellectual, social, emotional, and values development.

# The College Report Card
# for _____ College/University

### The Students

1. To what extent are you comfortable with the student body: intellectually, values, work/play balance, role of alcohol, etc. (Base your answers on what you've learned from all the sources in #3 above.)

### In The Classroom

2. What percentage of the typical freshman's class time is spent in classes of 30 or fewer students? (Ask students.)

3. What percentage of class time is spent in lecture versus active learning? (Ask students.)

   Most educators agree that learning is often enhanced when students are active; for example, participating in discussions, case studies, field studies, hands-on activities. It's tough to achieve active learning in an auditorium. It's particularly important that freshman classes be small because first-year students are just getting used to college-level work. Students who might be tempted to space out or even play hooky in a large lecture class should pay special attention to class size.

   Many colleges report a misleading statistic about class size: the faculty/student ratio. This statistic typically ranges from 1:10 to 1:25, even at huge state universities. Such numbers evoke images of classes of 10-25 students. The faculty/student ratio is deceptive because it often includes faculty who do research but never teach, or at least never teach undergraduates. The faculty/student ratio also includes courses that few freshmen take. What good is it that Medieval Horticulture has three students if Intro. to Anything has 300? Hence, the previous two questions are important.

4. Are there special programs that enable you to get many smaller classes; e.g., honors programs, college-within-a-college programs, living-learning centers? How are students selected for these programs? (Read college guides and admissions material.)

5. Are there normally enough sections of required courses to accommo-date the needs of all students? How easy is it to register for the class-es you want; e.g., do students register by telephone? (Ask students.)

6. What percentage of your instructors would you describe as inspira-tional? (Ask students.)

7. What letter grade would you give to the average instructor? (Ask students.)

8. Does the college make available to students a booklet summarizing student evaluations of faculty? (Ask students.)

   Such a booklet makes it much easier to find good instructors. Also, its presence suggests that the college is more concerned about stu-dent rights as a consumer than it is about covering up professors' failings.

9. In a typical introductory social science or humanities course, how many pages of writing are typically assigned? In an advanced class? (Ask students.)

10. Does feedback on written work typically include detailed sugges-tions for improvement or just a letter grade with a few words of feed-back? (Ask students.)

11. Must all assignments be individually done, or are there sufficient opportunities to do team projects? (Ask students.)

12. Is the institution strong in your major or interest? (Consult *The Fiske Guide to Colleges, How to Get an Ivy League Education at a State Univer-sity*, and *Rugg's Recommendations on the Colleges*. Examine the college catalog.

    Sit in on an advanced class in your prospective major, and after class talk with students. Ask an admissions officer. Speak with a represen-tative from the career center.)

### *Intellectual Life Outside The Classroom*

13. How good is the advising you've received? Is your advisor available when you need her or him? (Ask students.)

14. How easy is it to get to work on a faculty member's research project? (Ask students and faculty in your prospective major.)

    Working under a professor's wing is an excellent opportunity for active learning. Also, research is a central product of a college or uni-versity's efforts, so when students become part of the research effort, they feel more like members of the campus community.

15. To what extent do the viewpoints expressed on campus reflect true diversity rather than, for example, just the "politically correct" view or just the conservative stance? (Ask students and faculty.)

16. How frequently do faculty invite students to share a meal? (Ask students.)

17. How frequently do eminent speakers and artists appear on or near campus? (Ask anyone. Look at the student newspaper.)

18. If a Pulitzer Prize-winning author were to give a noontime lecture on campus, how many undergraduate students would show up? (Ask students.)

19. How much does the typical student study between Friday dinner and Sunday dinner? (Read college guides, ask students.)

20. Do faculty frequently attend meetings of student organizations? (Ask students, faculty.)

21. Do faculty live in student residence halls? Does it encourage good faculty-student interaction? (Call a residence hall front desk.)

Questions 22–26 in this section can probably be best answered by someone in the academic affairs office.]

22. How does the institution assess a prospective faculty member's ability to teach?

    Ideally, undergraduate institutions should require prospective undergraduate faculty members to submit a teaching portfolio consisting of videotapes of undergraduate classes, student evaluations, syllabi, and conduct a demonstration class at the freshman level. Many colleges only require prospective faculty to do a demonstration of a graduate level seminar in their research area. That says little about their ability to teach undergraduates.

23. How likely is it that a good teacher who teaches well but publishes little will be granted tenure?

24. On your most recent student satisfaction survey, what was the average rating for academic life? For out-of-classroom life?

    This is the equivalent of being able to ask hundreds of students how they like their college. If they say that the institution doesn't conduct student satisfaction surveys, it suggests that the institution doesn't care much about what students think.

25. How much money per student is spent annually on helping faculty to improve their teaching?

Colleges frequently espouse the importance of good teaching. The answer to this question lets you know if a college puts its money where its mouth is.

26. What is done to ensure that students receive high-quality advising?

   For example, do faculty get special training in how to advise students? Does advising count in faculty promotion decisions? Can students and advisors, via computer, see what courses the student has taken and still must take?

## Co-Curricular Life
27. Does the new-student orientation program extend beyond the traditional 1–3 days? (Ask students, consult admissions brochure and catalog.)

28. What percentage of freshmen, sophomores, juniors, and seniors can obtain on-campus housing? This affects campus community. (Consult admissions material, ask admissions or housing office.)

29. Describe residence hall life. How close is it to the living-learning environment described in admission brochures? (Ask students.)

30. How attractive is student housing? (Ask students. Tour facilities.)

31. How well did you like your freshman roommate? This item assesses the quality of the college's roommate-matching procedure. (Ask students.)

32. Rate the quality of extracurricular activities you care about; e.g., intramural basketball, varsity football, debate, dance, student newspaper, drama. (Read college guides, admissions materials. Ask students, tour facilities.)

33. Is the school's location a plus or minus? Why? (Read college guides, ask students.)

34. How many crimes were committed on or near campus last year? How many were violent? Are campus security efforts adequate? (Each college and university is required to provide you with a report on crime on campus, compiled based on federal guidelines. Also check local newspapers)

35. What is the quality of life for special constituencies; e.g., gay, adult, minority, or students with a disability? (Read admission materials, ask students, phone the office that serves that constituency.)

36. How strong is the sense of community and school spirit among the students? (Read college guides, ask students.)

37. In the dining hall, do students primarily eat in homogeneous groups: fraternity/sorority members, racial groups, etc. (Ask students, observe first-hand.)

38. How extensive are the opportunities for public service? (Ask students, the career center.)

### The "Real" World

39. How extensive are the internship opportunities?

   Internships embody active learning, allow students to bridge theory and practice, try out a career without penalty, and make job connections. (Ask students, contact the career center.)

40. How effective are the career planning and placement services?

   Most colleges offer some career planning and placement, but the best ones offer critiques of videotaped mock interviews, the SIGI or Discover computer career guidance systems, video-interviewing with distant employers, extensive counseling, many job listings, on-campus employee interviews, and extensive connections with alumni. (Ask students and personnel at the career center.)

41. In your field, what percentage of students get jobs or get accepted into graduate school? (Ask students, faculty in your prospective major, ask at the career center.)

### Overall Indicators Of The Institution's Quality

42. What percentage of incoming freshmen return for the sophomore year? (Consult college guides, ask admissions representative or call the office of institutional research.)

43. What should I know about the college that wouldn't appear in print? (Ask everyone.)

44. What's the best and worst thing about this college? (Ask everyone.)

45. In what ways is this college different from College X? Ask about a similar institution that you're considering. (Ask admissions representative, students, perhaps faculty.)

46. What sorts of students would be the perfect fit for this school? A poor fit? (Read college guides, ask everyone.)

47. What is the total cost of attending this college, taking into account the most likely financial aid package? (Ask the financial aid office.)

48. What other information about the school could affect your decision? e.g., beauty of campus, food, graduation requirements, percent of students of your religious or ethnic group. (Consult catalog, college guides, students, ask admissions representative.)

# 11

# HOW TO TEST-DRIVE A COLLEGE

*Martin Nemko*

College A or College B? A visit is key to deciding. You wouldn't buy a car without popping the hood and test-driving it. With a college, you're spending thousands of dollars and years of your life, so better take it for a good spin.

The trouble is, many students make a worse decision after a visit than they would have made without one. A college can feel so over-whelming that many students come away with little more than, "The campus was beautiful and the tour guide was nice."

Here's how to put a college through its paces.

## Preparing

1. Plan to visit when school is in session. Visiting a college when it isn't in session is like test-driving a car by seeing how the engine idles.

2. Call ahead. Ask the admissions office if you can spend the night in a residence hall, perhaps with a student in your prospective major. If you think it might help, make an appointment for an interview. Get directions to campus and a campus map. Also find out whether tours are given, and if so, where.

3. Reread the college guides. If you're just about to visit, that seemingly boring profile of a college should raise questions in your mind. Think

of yourself as a journalist. Make a list of probing questions based on the write-ups.

4. Review the questions on the College Report Card.

## The Visit

Write what you learn on the College Report Card. Especially if you're visiting more than one college, the differences among them can blur.

Here are the stops on my campus tour. If you're with parents, split up, at least for part of the time. Not only can you see more, but it's easier to ask questions like, "What's the social life like?"

### The Official Tour

Take the tour mainly to orient you to campus geography, not to help you pick your college. Tour guides are almost always enthusiastic. The tour guide, however, is usually a knowledgeable student and generally pretty candid. So while walking to the next point of interest, you may want to ask some questions.

### Grab Students

Select students who seem approachable in the plaza or student union and ask a question. Most love to talk about their school. You might start with, "What's it like to go to this school? What do you like and not like?"

In addition to students at random, athletes should query players on the team, oboists should quiz orchestra members. Consider dropping by a residence hall and talking with the student at the front desk. Or pay a visit to the student government or student newspaper office. Folks there know a lot about life on campus. While you're at the newspaper office, pick up a few copies of the student newspaper. What sorts of stories make the front page? What's in the letters to the editor?

Never leave a campus without talking with at least five people that the admissions staff did not put in front of you. As with anything else, some people will love the school and others will hate it, but talking with a good number of people should give you the information you need to "get the picture."

### A Dining Hall And/Or The Student Union

Sample the food. Tasty nuggets or chicken tetrachloride? Are you a vegetarian? See if there's more than a salad bar and cheese-drenched veggies. While you're in the dining hall (or in the student union), eavesdrop on discussions. Can you see yourself happily involved in such conversations?

Most colleges claim to celebrate diversity. The dining hall is a great place to assess the reality because, there, integration is voluntary. Do diverse groups of people eat together? Bulletin boards are windows to the soul of a college. What kind of information is posted on the bulletin boards?

### Sit In On A Class

Best choices are a class in your prospective major, a required class, or a special class you're planning to enroll in; for example, an honors class. At the break, or at the end of the class, ask students some questions. If it's a class in your prospective major, ask students how they like the major and what you should know about the major that might not appear in the catalog.

### How To Visit Several Classes In A Short Time

In addition to sitting in on one whole class, ask for the name of a building with many undergraduate classes. Walk down its halls and peek into open doors. What percentage of classes are alive and interactive? In what percentage is the professor droning on like a bored career bureaucrat?

Some students say that they are too shy to peek into or sit in on classes, but it's worth conquering the shyness. Shouldn't you look at a sample of classes before committing to years' worth?

### A Night In The Dorm

It's an uncomfortable thought. "I'm a high school kid. I'll feel weird spending a whole night with college students." Fortunately, it usually ends up being fun as well as informative. A bunch of students will probably cluster around you, dying to reveal the inside dirt. You'll also learn what the students are like: Too studious? Too raunchy? Too radical? Too preppy? At 10:30 P.M. on a weeknight, is the atmosphere "Animal House," an academic sweatshop, or a good balance? Are the accommodations plush or spartan? One prospective student found a dorm crawling with roaches. You won't get that information on the official tour.

### Beware Of Bias

We've already mentioned the peril of an overzealous tour guide. Here are other sources of bias in a college visit:

### Timing

You visited a college on Thursday at noon. That's when a college is at its best. Thousands of students are buzzing around amid folks hawking hand-crafted jewelry or urging you to join their clubs or causes, all perhaps accompanied by a rock band. But if you were to arrive at 4:30, even the most dynamic college won't seem as exciting.

### Weather

No matter how great the college, rain can't help but dampen enthusiasm for it.

### The Campus

Remember this saying, "Better good teachers in wooden buildings than wooden teachers in good buildings." As mentioned earlier, it's easy to be overwhelmed by ivy-covered buildings, lush lawns, and chiming bell towers. A beautiful campus is nice, but don't let it overwhelm other factors. Because colleges begin to melt together after awhile, you might want to take photos of each campus.

## After The Visit

Finish recording what you've learned on the College Report Card immediately after leaving campus. Especially if you've visited a number of colleges, it's easy to confuse key features of one with another: "Was it North Carolina-Asheville or St. John's that had great vegetarian food?" Probably, additional questions about each college will come to mind after you leave. Write them down and send them to your college interviewer as part of a thank you note which expresses your appreciation for the time spent and the advice you received.

## The Decision

After you get home, ask yourself these three questions:

- Would I be happy living and learning with these types of students until I graduate?
- Would I be happy being instructed by these professors?
- Would I be happy being in this environment for four years or more?

If it's yes to all three, you may have found your new home. Congratulations!

*Martin Nemko is the author of* How to Get an Ivy League Education at a State University, *which profiles the undergraduate programs at 115 public colleges and universities. His firm, Nemko & Associates, assists administrators in developing and evaluating undergraduate programs.*